Beginner's Guide to Golf

Written by

Larry Dennis

Published by

National Golf Foundation
1150 South U.S. Highway One, Suite 401
Jupiter, FL 33477

ACKNOWLEDGMENTS

The National Golf Foundation wishes to thank the following individuals for their involvement in the conception and development of this book:

Tom Addis, *Head PGA Professional, Singing Hills Country Club, El Cajon, Calif.*; **Ken Blanchard,** *author and lecturer*; **Peter Bonanni,** *Publishing Director, GOLF Magazine*; **Betsy Clark,** *Director of Education, LPGA*; **David Fay,** *Executive Director, USGA*; **Chester Gore,** *President, Chester Gore Co., New York, N.Y.*; **Mike Hebron,** *Head Professional, Smithtown Landing Golf Course (N.Y.) and the PGA of America's 1991 Teacher of the Year*; **Chuck Hogan,** *author and golf instructor*; **Tom Mayer,** *Spalding Sports Worldwide*; **Charley Stine,** *Editor-in-Chief, Golfweek*; **Gary Wiren,** *President, Golf Around the World*

Illustrations by Roy Doty
Cover design by Richard Munson

Publisher's Cataloging-in-Publication Data

Dennis, Larry, 1933-
    A beginner's guide to golf : how to get started, and have fun doing it / written by Larry Dennis. — Jupiter, FL : National Golf Foundation, ©1994

       p.:   ill.;   cm.
    Includes bibliographical references and index.
    ISBN: 0-9638647-0-X
    1. Golf.
I. Title
GV965.D46   1994
796.352 dc20   93-85975

Manufactured in the United States of America.

10 9 8 7 6 5 4 3

FOREWORD

By Arnold Palmer

I 've been lucky. I've been able to spend my life playing a game, the greatest game in the world. My father, Deacon, who was the professional and greenkeeper at Latrobe Country Club in Pennsylvania, made a special set of golf clubs for me when I was three years old, and I've been hooked ever since.

Golf has given me almost everything I have. I met my wife, Winnie, at a golf tournament. I've made a very good living playing the game and have built successful businesses because of it. I've made many friends, some rich and powerful, some just friends who have remained friends for life.

All that is important, but it's not really the point. I love to play golf. I would have played golf every chance I got if I had been a manufacturer's representative all my life, which in fact is what I was, just before turning pro. The lucky part is that I could make golf my life's work.

Work is not the word. Golf has always been play for me. It still is. Even if you take the game seriously, as most of us do, it's still just a game. It's just play. That's why I'm still playing tournament golf. I don't always play as well as I'd like—none of us do. But I still enjoy the game and the challenge. And when I go home, I play golf with my friends. It's fun.

I've been given some credit for helping touch off the explosion in golf's popularity back in the '50s and '60s, but I'm not sure I deserve that. I think golf, with or without me or anyone else, would have become as popular as it is today simply because of what it is.

Golf is a game that is deceptively simple and endlessly complicated. It's a game that no one has ever really conquered, and no one ever will. That's what makes it intriguing and so much fun. It's a game that lets you enjoy other people. You have partners and you have opponents. You play with both and they don't become your enemies. They become your friends.

It's not a sport for which you have to qualify to play. Anybody can go play it. That's one of the things that makes it the best game there is.

My golf course design company creates courses with that in mind. I suppose it's important that a course be difficult for the best players. But it's more important that it be playable for a husband and wife and their children, so they can go out and enjoy it. That's what golf is all about. It's not about the professional tours. It's about you and your friends.

You probably never will make your living at golf. Very few do. Very few want to. But you can have a lifetime of fun at it. If this book helps you do that, as I think it will, then you will be as lucky as I have been.

INTRODUCTION

This book is about how to begin playing the game of golf and how to enjoy playing it the rest of your life. If you are a new golfer or an infrequent golfer, there is something in here to help you get comfortable in the game and begin to love it. If you have already become an avid player, there is something here that will make you love it even more.

This book is about fun, because that's what golf is. It will tell you about golf's charms and its pitfalls, both of which make it so appealing to such a broad range of the human race (and maybe others, for all anybody knows).

This book will tell you how to get started, the best ways to learn how to *play*—and the word is emphasized, you'll note. It will tell you how to buy clubs and the other gear you need to play the game. You'll find out how a golf operation works, the different kinds of facilities, the personnel who work there, the costs and how you can get involved in the fun of golf.

You'll learn the things everybody should know about the game, starting with an explanation of a golf course, its design and its parts. You'll get the basic rules of etiquette and play and an explanation of the handicap system, how it works and why it makes golf unique. There's a chapter on the language of the game and the derivation of some of its colorful terms so you can "talk golf" with the best of them. There's a chapter on the games golfers play that make the game even more fun, and there's a collection of other information that will help you get easily into the playing mode.

Should you wish to know more about any of the aspects of the game covered in this book, you'll find references to other recommended reading at the end of most chapters.

In the meantime, this book will have served it's purpose if it simply increases your understanding of why 25 million Americans and millions more around the world know what we're talking about when we say that golf is truly a game of a lifetime.

Joseph F. Beditz
President & CEO
National Golf Foundation

CONTENTS

Acknowledgments ii

Foreword iii

Introduction v

CHAPTER 1   —   Golf...The Game 1

CHAPTER 2   —   The History of an Ancient Game 5

CHAPTER 3   —   How to Get Started 11

CHAPTER 4   —   Learning the Golf Swing 19

CHAPTER 5   —   What You Should Know About a Golf Course 33

CHAPTER 6   —   How Golf Courses Operate 39

CHAPTER 7   —   Equipment—How and What to Buy 45

CHAPTER 8   —   How to Play Safely, Courteously and Quickly 51

CHAPTER 9   —   The Rules of the Game 57

CHAPTER 10   —   The Handicap and Slope Systems 65

CHAPTER 11   —   Other Things You Should Know 71

CHAPTER 12   —   Games Golfers Play 79

CHAPTER 13   —   The Language of Golf 85

CHAPTER 14   —   The Joy is in the Experience 91

APPENDIX   —   Listing of Golf Schools 95

GOLF...THE GAME

Mark Twain once described golf as a walk in the park spoiled, or words to that effect. Mark, of course, was wrong. Golf does not spoil anything. It enhances. A golf course enhances the environment. The game enhances the player....at least in most cases.

Golf can be hellish, and it can be heavenly. It can be frustrating, even exasperating, some of the time. But, probably because of those bouts of frustration, it can be the most rewarding game on earth.

At the very least, golf is intriguing. With some (probably most of us if we would only admit it) it is addictive. It's an addiction that is not damaging to your health and can be controlled....most of the time. But once you catch the fever, it rarely goes entirely away.

Golf's inherent charm is that it's a challenge, perhaps the ultimate challenge in the world of games, not only to your physical skills but to your mental and emotional faculties. It tells you what you are and who you are. It brings out the best, and sometimes the worst, in a player. There is a saying that you can learn more about a person on the golf course than anywhere else, and nobody close to the game would doubt that.

Sam Snead, who played the game as well as any half dozen men in history, once said that he had tried most of the sports and that golf was by far the most difficult to play. But in this very difficulty lies the hook. Nobody masters the game. You only come as close as you can, on any given shot or any given day. The perfect shot seems always to

Once you catch the fever, it never goes away entirely.

be tantalizingly just out of reach. And when it happens, as it does occasionally, it goes away again, and the quest begins anew. It is this quest that begets the addiction.

Most of all, and because of all this, golf is fun....immeasurably so. The well-smashed drive, the crisp iron to the green, the well-laid pitch, the long putt that topples in the hole—or the short putt, for that matter—bring moments of bliss perhaps unmatched in sport, moments that erase from memory the shots that didn't go as planned. In its raw form, golf pits the player against the elements and the course. There is no help. And golf, because of its playing fields, is sometimes not fair. Sometimes the breaks go against you, sometimes for you. At the end of the day you add up your score and, more important, reflect on how *you* did against this unfathomable opponent, how well you controlled yourself, how well you thought, how well you performed. That's the essence of the joy and the fun in the game.

You indeed can play golf by yourself and enjoy it. You can play with your peers and enjoy it. You can play with your family. Thanks to golf's unique handicap system, you can play with the best players in the world or the worst and have an enjoyable competition. And you can do this all your life, as a youngster or an oldster and for all the years in between.

Golf's playgrounds, its courses, separate this game from others. They are built near oceans and lakes, rivers and streams, across sandy dunesland, in deserts and jungles, on mountains, through towering forests and across lush meadows, each course unique in its own way. Some may be "better" than others, whatever that means. There is always great delight in this ever-changing variety.

Golf is healthy, especially for the walker. Don't let anyone tell you that tramping five or six miles over any terrain won't reduce the waistline and improve your mental outlook. Golf is a delight to the senses. Teeing off in the early day with the sun glinting off the dew and the smell of new-mown grass in the air, or playing a few quiet holes in the evening with the shadows lengthening, or even facing howling seaside winds or battling a cold rain....it all makes the challenge even greater and the satisfaction sweeter. It's why more than 25 million people of all ages in the United States today play golf.

It's why you should too.   ■

Other Publications

If you would like to know more about what's covered in this chapter, here is some additional suggested reading.

Golf in the Kingdom (Michael Murphy, Hardcover, Published 1993 by Ten Speed Press)

The Mystery of Golf (Arnold Hultain, Hardcover, Published 1987 by Classics of Golf))

Mostly Golf: A Bernard Darwin Anthology (Peter Ryde [Editor], Hardcover, Published 1989 by Classics of Golf)

Hints on Golf (Horace Hutchinson, Hardcover, Published 1987 by Classics of Golf))

THE HISTORY OF
AN ANCIENT GAME

T he beginnings of golf are lost in time. There are records of
various games using clubs and balls having been played
throughout the centuries, by the Romans, the Dutch and
others. Most evidence points to Scotland as the country of origin and
to St. Andrews as the first real golf course.

Robert Trent Jones, the noted golf course architect, theorizes
that the game began, perhaps in the early 1400s, when sailors
docking at the port of St. Andrews broke up the monotony of the two-
mile walk to town by swinging sticks at rocks. The man who got there
in the fewest strokes was the winner.

Whether this is accurate, there is a recorded sale of a golf ball in
Scotland in 1452, and in 1457 James II of Scotland banned "fut ball
and golfe" on the grounds the games were luring the country's
archers away from their practice. It was banned again in 1491 by
James IV and stiff penalties for violations were imposed.

It must have been about this time, however, that King James
himself fell under golf's spell. It is recorded that he played golf in
1502, shortly after he signed a perpetual peace treaty between
Scotland and England and announced his forthcoming marriage to
Princess Margaret, the daughter of England's King Henry VII. It was
a peace that lasted only 11 years, but it served to introduce golf to
England. The game continued to flourish in Scotland, and when
James VI of Scotland ascended the throne of England as James I in
1603, he brought the game to a popularity in that country that has
never waned.

Then, as now, it was a game for commoners and kings. At first there were no official rules, and the number of holes on a course varied with the amount of land available. It wasn't until the 18th century that golf began to take shape as it exists today. In 1744, the Company of Gentleman Golfers, now the Honourable Company of Edinburgh Golfers, was formed for the purpose of holding an annual competition on the links of Leith. Now housed at the great Muirfield links outside Edinburgh, this was probably the first golf club. It was followed by the Society of St. Andrews Golfers in 1754, which in 1834 by decree of William IV became the Royal and Ancient Society. St. Andrews became the accepted home of the game and remains so today.

The first balls were "featheries," made of feathers stuffed into a pocket of leather, and clubs came in all shapes, sizes and materials. The feathery yielded to the gutta-percha ball or "gutty" in the 1840s, which in turn gave way to the rubber Haskell ball around the turn of the century. The history of balls and clubs used in golf is almost as fascinating as the game itself, one that continues to delight collectors of the artifacts. So, too, does the literature of golf. No other sport has such a rich and diverse library devoted to it.

Golf comes to America

There is evidence that golf, or a form of it, was played in America in the Low Country of South Carolina and Georgia as early as the 1700s. The Royal Montreal Golf Club was formed in 1873, making it the first on this continent. The game was played for awhile in western Pennsylvania, near Foxburg, and in 1884 the Oakhurst Club was founded in West Virginia. That club soon disappeared, however, and credit for bringing the game to this country generally goes to John Reid, a transplanted Scot living in Yonkers, N.Y. In late 1887 he had some clubs and balls imported from St. Andrews in Scotland. The next spring he and some pals laid out a rudimentary three-hole course, and in the fall they formed the St. Andrew's Golf Club, the first such club to endure. Thus the Apple Tree Gang, as the group came to known, was born, and so was golf, officially, in the United States.

It has grown unchecked ever since. Clubs began to spring up, especially in the northeast and as far west as Chicago. In December of 1894, representatives of five clubs—St. Andrew's, Shinnecock Hills on Long Island, the Newport Country Club in Rhode Island, The Country Club near Boston and Chicago Golf Club—met and formed

*Legend has it that the King of Scotland once banned golf
because it was luring the nation's archers away from practice.*

what became the United States Golf Association, whose purpose was
to conduct national championships and, eventually, to defend the
integrity of the game.

The first heroes of golf in this country were mostly immigrants
from Scotland and England who were more familiar with the game.
But soon native-born players began to dominate. John McDermott
became the first American to win the U.S. Open in 1911. In 1913,
Francis Ouimet, an amateur and former caddie, shocked the golf
world by beating England's Harry Vardon and Ted Ray in a playoff for
the Open title at The Country Club. That touched off an explosion in
popularity that has taken us through the eras of Walter Hagen and
Gene Sarazen, of Bobby Jones, of Ben Hogan, Byron Nelson, Sam
Snead, Babe Didriksen Zaharias, Patty Berg and Louise Suggs, of
Arnold Palmer, Jack Nicklaus, Gary Player, Mickey Wright and Betsy
Rawls, of Kathy Whitworth, Carol Mann, JoAnne Carner, Lee Trevino
and Tom Watson and on to today's legions of great players.

A game of wide appeal

The game has always been played in high places, which probably
helped it become a game of the people. President William Howard Taft

Golf's no stranger to the White House.

was an avid golfer. Palmer, with his slashing style and charismatic personality, certainly raised the game to new heights of popularity in the late 1950s and early '60s. But just as much credit should go to President Dwight D. Eisenhower, who became the most visible golfer in the country at the same time Palmer was tearing up the professional tour. And George Bush, whose grandfather, George Herbert Walker, was once president of the USGA and donated the trophy for the Walker Cup Match, kept the game in the presidential spotlight, as does Bill Clinton today.

It also doesn't hurt that golf has now become the game of choice among all kinds of celebrities, in sports, in entertainment and in just about every field you can imagine. Fans across the country agonize over actor Jack Lemmon's annual attempt to make the cut at the AT&T Pro-Am, just as they ponder Michael Jordan's announced intent to play the pro tour after his basketball career is over.

The popularity of golf in the United States is at a record high....and continues to rise. More than one in 10 Americans play the game, and more than two million try it for the first time each year. Equipment continues to improve and golf courses, from design and maintenance standpoints, are getting much better. Most important, golf is growing because it is more accessible to the public than ever before. It is no longer a game for the wealthy male sequestered in his private club....hasn't been for a long time, in fact. Nearly 65 percent of the more than 14,000 golf courses in existence in this country are open to the public, and 70 percent of all rounds are played at public facilities. And women comprise one of the fastest-growing segments of the golf population.

It has truly become, and will remain, a game for all and a game for a lifetime. ■

Other Publications

If you would like to know more about what's covered in this chapter, here is some additional suggested reading.

A Golfer's Companion: The World of Golf and a Personal Record Book (Michael Hobbs, Hardcover, Published 1997 by Lorenz Books)

Golf in America: The First 100 Years (George Peper, Hardcover, Published 1994 by Abradale Press)

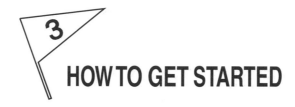

HOW TO GET STARTED

S everal years ago, shortly after taking up golf in earnest, my wife, Lynn, played in her first Ladies Day event at our club. "I was so nervous on the first tee that I almost threw up," she reported later. However, she recovered nicely from the experience. Three years later she was the club champion and today carries a single digit handicap.

Chuck Hogan, a teacher training specialist and president of Sports Enhancement Associates in Sedona, Arizona, says the biggest problem facing the beginning golfer, or the relatively new golfer, is worrying about what others will think. It can be a problem, in fact, for golfers at all levels.

"What will they think of me?" he says. "That's the one source of pressure for all golfers, at the tour level or the beginning level. You only put pressure on yourself by considering what others will think of you. It's a matter of self-image."

It's also a fact that simply getting into golf can be worrisome for the novice....how to do it, where to go, who to see? The process *can* be downright intimidating, although it shouldn't be and needn't be. It's a matter of knowing what to do.

About 70 percent of new golfers take up the game because they were introduced to it by family or friends. That makes the whole business a lot easier. Still, that leaves 30 percent of the new golfers who did it on their own, plus a huge, untapped well of would-be players who never really get into golf because of the above reasons or others.

That's sad, because the challenges involved in starting to play golf and continuing to play at the novice level are microscopic in comparison with the pleasure to be had from the game. If you don't play golf, or at least give it a very good try, you have overlooked a lot of fun for the rest of your life.

However it happened, we'll assume you have had some exposure to golf and decided that you might want to try the game, else you wouldn't be reading these words now. Welcome aboard. This book, and especially this chapter, is designed to help the beginner overcome the hurdles, real or imagined, that must be cleared to become a golfer. It will help the infrequent golfer do the same and indeed can be of help to any golfer short of Tour level. It might even teach some of those players a thing or two.

No reason for anxiety

Let's look first at what others might think of you, because you're concerned about that. The truth is, they're probably not going to think about you at all. And don't let that be a blow to your ego. Most, if not all, golfers you will meet and play with are too concerned with their own games to worry about yours. Moreover, they will probably applaud your efforts.

I have a friend, Dr. Dennis Colonello, who recently took up golf and is learning on the public courses in Los Angeles. Being paired with other golfers has been a pleasure, he tells me.

"Golfers appreciate someone who is learning," he says, "because all golfers are always in a learning mode. I've found that the tolerance level of the people I play with is phenomenal. They're patient, and they praise me when I hit a good shot."

So your companions won't think less of you as a person because you're hitting some wild shots. Everybody who plays the game has gone through the same learning experience....and has had fun doing it. Bad shots are part of the game, even for the best players in the world.

Chuck Hogan points out that the three most important things for the beginner, or any golfer, are that he or she plays *safely, courteously* and *quickly*. If you can meet those criteria, you can feel comfortable on any golf course. Read on and I'll tell you how do to that, no matter your level of skill.

You're never too young or too old to begin playing golf.

Those are really the only criteria. Age is not a factor. You're never too young or too old to begin playing golf. Gender, race, religion and level of athletic ability do not enter in. There are great athletes who play golf, some better than others, and there are many of us who can barely walk and chew gum at the same time who enjoy the game, each at our own levels. Even the condition of your bank account is not a critical factor. Prices vary widely. In some circles, golf is downright costly. But if your wallet doesn't allow you to travel in those circles, you can find an affordable way to play, which is kind of the way it is in any other sport and in life itself. The reward is the same.

First you have to find a way to get started, or to continue if you have already had some exposure to the game. Easy does it is the theme here. Find out what golf is all about before you leap with both feet and find that you might be in over your head. It is this factor, probably more than any other, that discourages the new golfer and makes him or her give up the game. Don't let that happen to you.

If you don't have a family member or friend who has been urging you to try golf, find someone else who can help. Seek advice from a friend or co-worker who plays golf. Drop in at a nearby public course and talk to the professional. He should be happy to give you direction. You're a potential customer.

Golf has plenty of "bunny slopes"

There are several types of golf facilities that can help you get into the games as easily as possible, starting with a miniature golf course. If there is one near you, give it a try. It's fun and can give you a feel for putting, which may be the most important part of the game anyway.

Next is the practice or driving range. This can be a stand-alone facility or part of a golf course. Almost all practice ranges and public courses are listed in the Yellow Pages of your telephone directory. Ideally you can find one that includes a putting green and an area for chipping, pitching and sand play—the short shots that help you learn the game easier and quicker. Most practice ranges and public

Golf ranges are an excellent place to get started.

courses that have practice areas offer rental clubs. Rent a couple, a driver and and a five-iron, for example, or borrow some from a friend. Whack a few buckets of balls, just trying to get your shots in the air and going generally in the right direction.

The correct way to learn is by taking lessons from a professional. It will speed the process, ease the frustration and more quickly let you experience the satisfaction of good shots. But if you feel you are not quite ready for that step, read the basic instruction in Chapter 4 on how to hold the club and stand to the ball. That's all you need for the moment. Then just go hit a few. Chances are you'll hit enough good ones to bring you back. After all, we're never potentially worse than our best shot.

Although the process of getting started can be downright intimidating, it needn't be.

You can even practice at home

Actually, you can learn a lot about how to hit a golf ball in your own back yard or on your living room carpet. Find a couple of clubs and a putter, the club that is used to roll the ball on the green. You can buy plastic practice balls at almost any sporting goods store or golf discount store. They don't travel very far and you can't break anything with them, but they simulate real flight. And buy a sleeve of three real balls with which you can practice your putting indoors. You may be surprised at how quickly you get the hang of it.

Before you set foot on a golf course, read Chapters 8 and 9. They deal with the etiquette of golf and the rules of the game in simple terms. This will help you learn how to get around a course competently before you ever start.

Par-3 courses are great places to begin playing real golf. These are courses made up entirely of short holes, ranging in length from under 100 yards to perhaps 200 yards. Each hole is designed to be reached, ideally, in one stroke. There are more than 700 of these courses in the country open to the public, some of them lighted for night play. If there is one near you, give it a whirl. The rules of golf and golf course etiquette still apply, but because there is less necessity to hit the ball a long way there will be less pressure on you and you can play more quickly. Learning the shorter shots also will help you immensely when you get on a regulation-length course.

The executive course is a step up from the par-3 layout. Usually it is made up of a number of par-3 and par-4 holes. The latter are designed to be reached in two strokes, so now your longest shots often are required from the tee. While there normally are no monstrously long par-4s on an executive course, quite often the design is testing enough to challenge the skills of any player. This is real golf on a slightly reduced scale. There are more than 800 of them in the U.S., and they are popular because they require less land, can be played in a shorter time and still demand all the skills needed on a regulation course.

Moving out onto the regulation length course

The regulation course is just that, one that has a full complement of par-3, par-4 and par-5 holes of varying lengths. A course usually is made up of 18 holes, although in earlier times there were many nine-hole courses in existence, and a few are still being built today. No one quite knows why 18 is the magic number. One legend has it that the ancient Scot could get 18 swigs from a bottle of whisky, one per hole, and when the bottle was finished so was he. That theory is unverified, however. St. Andrews, the cradle of golf in Scotland, once was a 12-hole layout until it was redesigned.

A full 18-hole course usually will measure between 5,000 and 5,500 yards from the forward tees and from about 6,000 to 7,000 from the middle and back tees. That kind of flexibility in course design is one factor that makes golf a wonderful game for all, because you can play it at a length best suited to your abilities.

The fact that there are 18 holes on a golf course doesn't mean you have to play them all, especially at first. Remember, you're taking it slowly as you learn this game. Play just nine holes if you like, or even fewer. Most public courses have nine-hole fees for late-afternoon play.

Try to find a time when the course is not crowded, if that's possible. Late evening or very early in the morning, if the facility allows it, is usually best. Ask the professional staff for advice on the best time to play.

Play with a friend or play by yourself. You might have to wait a bit if there are groups ahead of you, but you can use the time to practice your swing or hit extra shots, as long as you don't hold up players behind you.

As a beginning or infrequent golfer, you're just trying to get comfortable on the course. Score is not important right now. Learn to swing a club, learn to play shots and learn how to conduct yourself on a golf course. If you get a little frustrated, or if the group behind is crowding you, pick up your ball and go to the next hole. Things will get better. Eventually you will start concentrating on your score, although in the long run that's never the most important factor, at least until you get good enough for tournament competition.

The fun comes from the doing and from being on a beautiful playground, right from the start. The satisfaction grows as you get better at it. ■

Other Publications

If you would like to know more about what's covered in this chapter, here is some additional suggested reading.

Playing the Great Game of Golf: Making Every Minute Count (Ken Blanchard, Published 1992 by William Morrow & Co.)

LEARNING THE GOLF SWING

I t's important to learn how to swing a golf club to the best of your ability. It's a hundred times more important to learn how to play golf.

In his book *Learning Golf,* Chuck Hogan says, "Golf swing is golf swing. It is something to learn in preparation to play golf. It certainly isn't golf. Your awareness is not devoted to a target. Your attention is focused on some mechanical or biophysical motion which attempts to satisfy some or all notions of how to swing."

On the other hand, Hogan says, "Actual golf is the adventure of being on the golf course. A golf shot is the interaction with a target and its conditions. You are a part of those conditions…a piece of the activity. You are playing golf when being absorbed in the interaction of literally playing with and through the target…"

When you play golf, he says, just play golf. Hit the ball, as best you can, to the target. Chase the ball and do it again. The golf course is made for golfing, so *play* golf.

Dr. Bob Rotella, a sports psychologist at the University of Virginia, says, "We have to educate people that there's a difference between working on the swing and playing golf. We've educated the public into thinking that the great professional players are out on the course working on six different swing thoughts. They're not. They're playing golf."

Hogan compares the process to learning to type, or learning to drive a car, or learning to write. You learn the mechanics step by step, internalizing them until you don't have to think about them when you are performing the actual process.

In their book *How to Become a Complete Golfer*, noted teachers Bob Toski and Jim Flick emphasize the "whole-part-whole learning" process in which the concept of the whole swing is explained, the parts are taught separately and then are put back together into a whole swing. In essence, that's what Hogan and Rotella are saying, too.

Above all ... golf is first a game

Even though some of us get pretty serious about it—too serious, probably—golf is really just a game. Games are to *play*, not to work at. That holds true whether you're on the golf course trying to advance the ball to your target or on the practice range learning the mechanics that will help you do that better.

Tom Kite, the 1992 U.S. Open champion and golf's all-time leading money-winner, has had a reputation throughout his career as a man who works hard on his game. In his book, *How to Play Consistent Golf*, Kite pooh-poohs that notion.

"People talk about how hard Tom Kite *works* on his game, and that's not true," he says. "Tom Kite *plays* at his game. When I go to the practice tee, I play practice. When I go to the golf course, I play golf.

"Practice was never work when I was growing up, and it's not work now. Even when I'm hitting the ball poorly and get frustrated, it's not work. It's fun to try to put the puzzle together. I love to practice, and I think the thing that made me enjoy it so much was the approach Mr. (Harvey) Penick (Kite's long-time teacher) took. He invented games for us to play on the practice tee. We played golf on the golf course and we played practice on the practice tee. And it was wonderful. You're never impatient, it's never work, when you're having fun. The more fun you can have, the more creative you are and the better job you do. And you never get tired. I do better when I take that approach, and you will, too."

The upshot of all this is that both learning to swing and learning to play should be fun. And it will be if you take this approach. You'll also get better at both much faster. This philosophy, incidentally, is effective for players at any level. If it's good enough for Tom Kite, it's good enough for the rest of us.

Golf is essentially a simple game that often is made far too

Learning to swing and learning to play can and should both be fun.

complicated. True, it is played on holes and courses that are never the same, where each shot is a little different than the preceding one. It is played under all kinds of weather conditions that affect those shots and require constant adjustment. And it is played with what, to the beginner at least, appears to be a bewildering variety of implements. Actually, it is this very inconstancy that makes golf the most challenging and the most fun of all games.

Where we usually foul it up is in our approach to coping with all these variables. And almost always that fouling-up process starts with the swing and how we learn it....or don't learn it. We forget that the swing itself is basically a simple move and that every shot in golf, from the short putt to the long drive, is made with the same simple concept—you swing the club back and you swing it through to advance the ball toward the target. We get too wrapped up in the mechanics, the parts of the swing. We think too much about the path of the swing, the plane of the swing, the shifting of the weight, the cocking and uncocking of the wrists, keeping the left arm straight, keeping the head down or keeping it up. We think so much about the parts that we can never meld them into a whole, a swing that we can *feel* and use on the golf course while we are *playing* golf.

Whether you're a beginner or an advanced player, don't let that happen to you. Have fun building and refining your swing on the practice range. When you get to the first tee, have fun using whatever swing you have at the moment to play to the best of your abilities.

Getting professional help can save time and money

There are many ways to learn a golf swing. Trial and error is one of them. Learning from a friend is another. So is learning from your husband or your wife (although that sometimes is a sure road to divorce). But the best and surest way is to first learn the fundamentals of holding the club and standing to the ball through lessons from a qualified professional. It may seem like a little trouble at the time, and it will cost you money, but in the long run it will make your golfing life more enjoyable.

In the remainder of this chapter, then, you'll get a few simple guidelines on how to hold the club and how to stand to the ball. This is pretty boring stuff, and it takes longer than you may think necessary, but please pay attention to the details. They are important to the long-term health of your swing. And I promise you it's the only technical stuff in this book.

I'll then give you a simple concept of the swing, and I'll advise you on how to choose a professional and how to get the most out of his instruction. I'll also tell you where else to look for material that can help you learn.

And always remember that learning to swing a club is not the same as learning to play golf. The swing is only a component of golf, a means to an end. The end is having fun by *playing* golf, advancing the ball around the course by whatever means you have at your disposal on any given day.

How to hold the club

In the long run, holding the club properly may be the most important thing you learn about swinging a golf club. Because your hands are your only connection to the club, a good swing depends on them being placed on the club correctly. A good grip allows the hands to work together as a unit as you swing the club freely back and forward around your body. It gives you the best chance of returning the clubface square at impact so your shots have a better chance of going toward your target.

There is no one right grip for everybody. Hand size and physical structure vary with all of us. But there are some basic guidelines. Start with them and refine them as you get more into the learning process.

First, the right hand goes on the club below the left. There have been some good "cross-handed" golfers, but not many. (If you are a lefthander, of course, this and all the instruction that follows should be reversed.)

The club is held in the left hand with a combination of the fingers and the palm. The handle or grip end of the club should rest underneath the heel pad of the hand, running diagonally toward the base of the forefinger. The fingers then are closed around the handle, the thumb sitting slightly to the left side of that handle.

VARDON OR
OVERLAPPING

To position the right hand, place the roots of the first three fingers against the handle, which rests snugly against the callous pads. When you close the fingers, the groove between the heel and thumb pads of the right hand should fit snugly against the right thumb. The right forefinger should be slightly triggered and the thumb should sit slightly to the left side of the handle.

There are four grip variations you should know about. The little finger of the right hand can hook around the left forefinger, resting in the groove between that and the left index finger. That's known as the Vardon or overlap grip and is the most commonly used. It is named for Harry Vardon, the great English player early in this century. He popularized it, although it actually was first used by James Laidlaw, another Englishman.

INTERLOCKING

The second variation is the interlocking grip, in which the little finger of the right hand is hooked under the forefinger of the left, resting between the forefinger and the index finger. This has been mainly used by players with smaller hands, but it is strictly a matter of preference, what feels comfortable to you. Kite and a fellow named Jack Nicklaus both use the interlocking grip, so it's obviously effective.

The third variation is the full-fingered grip, in which all four fingers of the right hand are placed on

TEN FINGER
OR UNLAP

the handle, the little finger resting snugly against the left forefinger. This grip promotes greater flexibility in the hands and wrists and may be used effectively by the weaker player who needs to generate more clubhead speed.

A fourth variation, called the "reverse overlap," is used by most players in putting. In this one all the fingers of the right hand are placed on the club and the forefinger of the left hand either hooks around or is placed straight down against the fingers of the right. This simply places the hands a little closer together and tends to keep the wrists firmer, which is what you want during the putting stroke.

Whichever variation you use, the two hands should rest on the club approximately parallel to each other, the back of the left hand and the palm of the right facing in the general direction of your target.

How to stand to the ball

Setting up properly to give yourself the best chance to make a good swing involves several elements—*aim, stance (the position of your feet), the position of the ball in relation to your feet and posture, which is how you arrange the parts of your body as you are standing to the ball.* These preswing fundamentals are critically important, to the beginner or the best players in the world. Most bad shots, especially as a player's skill increases, are caused by doing something wrong before the swing even starts.

Remember, I'll just give you the basics here. As you learn and grow in the game and want to improve your swing and your play, which you will, you probably will want to make some adjustments to accommodate your physical characteristics and how you want to strike the ball. It's almost always best to make these refinements under the eye of a competent professional. Not only can a professional suggest what to do, he or she can watch to see that you are doing it. We cannot see ourselves as we stand to the ball and swing.

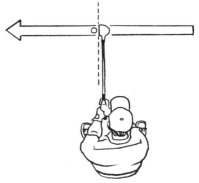

Aiming the club—As a basic rule, your clubface should be aimed squarely at your target or down the line on which you want your ball to start. This means the clubface will be perpendicular to that line. There will come a time when you will want to vary the clubface position at address to intentionally curve your shots, but trying to hit it straight is

Always make sure the clubface is aimed squarely at the target.

always a good place to start. As you set up to the ball, aim the club first, then set your body so it is aligned in the same direction the clubface is looking.

Stance—Stand so you are comfortably balanced. The usual guideline is to place your feet shoulder-width apart, measured from the insides of your heels. That can vary with the club you are swinging and the distance you want to hit the ball. It also can vary with your build and your ability to make a good turn back and through during the swing. Experiment to find the width that lets you do that and remain in balance. Your weight should be equally distributed between the balls and heels of the feet. You might want to turn the left foot outward or toward the target a little to help you swing more freely.

Feet should be shoulder-width apart.

Ball position—The ball is usually played from about two inches inside the left heel (away from the target) with the driver and is moved progressively back toward the center of the stance as the club in your hands gets shorter. Again, depending on your build and your flexibility, you may want to make adjustments, so experiment until you find a comfortable position with the various clubs. The direction the ball starts and how it curves often is a result of where it is played in your stance, so be sure to look at ball position if you are having problems.

Posture—This is pretty simple but very important. Take your stance, your weight balanced left and right, and flex your knees slightly, just enough to remove the tension. Bend from your hips so your arms are hanging naturally and the club is soled correctly—that means the bottom of the club is flat on the ground from toe to heel (front to back). As you bend, keep your back and neck in a relatively straight line, your head erect. How far you bend from the hips

Bend from the hips so your arms hang down naturally.

depends on the length of the club you're using. Don't worry about it. It will happen naturally.

When you assume this position, make sure all parts of your body—feet, knees, hips, shoulders and eyes—are set on lines parallel to your target line. This is the basic "square" position. As your play and your shotmaking goals become more sophisticated, you may vary this occasionally, but learn this setup position first.

Practice placing your hands on the club correctly. Practice standing to the ball in the correct position. Do it in front of a mirror so you can see what's happening. Practice until these positions become habit and you can *feel* them rather than having to think about assuming them. This may seem like a terrible waste of time, because you're not getting to bash that ball, which is what everybody wants to do. Trust me—if you do the right things before you swing the club back, you're 90 percent of the way to a good shot.

A final word on getting ready for your swing—*relax!* The club should be held lightly, using just enough pressure to control it throughout the swing. At the address position your muscles should be relaxed, with just enough tautness to let you make an athletic move with your swing. Golf is not an exercise in weightlifting. Seymour Dunn, one of the early and great players and teachers, said golf should be played in a state of grace. So play it gracefully and easily, and you'll play it much better.

How to swing

A first word on swinging a golf club—*re-read the preceding paragraph.* The golf swing should be easy and graceful. The easier you swing the faster you'll swing and the farther and straighter the ball will go. That sounds like a contradiction, but it's not. The muscles perform better and faster when they are relaxed than when they are tense. Resist the impulse to *hit* the ball. Just *swing through it,* and watch your shots fly the way you want them to.

How do you swing a golf club? The same way you swing anything else. Every shot in golf, from the shortest putt to the drive, is made with a swing that is simply back and through. Only the length varies. Going back, swing your hands and arms and the club back, around your body and up as your body turns away from the target. On the forward swing, your body turns toward the target as your hands and arms swing the club through the ball, around your body and up. Your weight goes to the side away from the target on the backswing, returning to the target side on the forward swing. Finish in a relaxed, straight-up position, facing your target with your weight almost totally on your left foot.

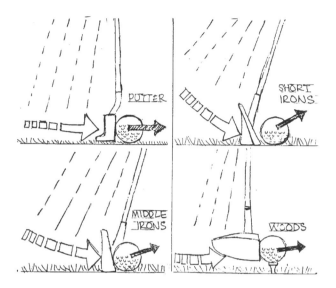

Different clubs require different strokes. Generally speaking, the lower lofted clubs require more of a sweeping motion.

Ever swing a baseball bat or a softball bat? The golf swing is the same motion in a different plane. Swing a few times at an imaginary ball fixed at waist level. Swing a few more times, gradually lowering the imaginary ball until it is on the ground. That's your golf swing.

Learning follows a model. Ideally you should pick someone—a good amateur, a professional, a tour player—whose size and physical characteristics are similar to yours. Perhaps buy an instruction video by a compatible player and just watch the swing. Or tape some golf tournaments on your VCR until you find a swing that you like and that fits you. Study the model.

Then practice repeating the model's swing, without variation, until you can *feel* it without having to think about it, until it becomes a habit. Swing without a ball at first. Just develop the feel of the swing. When you start swinging at a ball, don't worry about where it goes. Just feel the swing. Swing in a leisurely manner, back and through. Don't be in a hurry to hit the ball. It isn't going anywhere until you strike it. Then start paying attention to making contact on the ball with the center of the clubface. Feel the swing and feel the solid contact. You'll know when that happens and when it doesn't.

That's all you need to know about the swing at first. Eventually you can introduce variations from the model that you'll need to play off different lies and under different weather and turf conditions. But your basic swing should remain the same. Never get so far away from your swing model that you can't get back.

Sound pretty simple? It is. Leave it at that. Don't clutter your mind with technique, with different positions and movements, until you are advanced enough to comprehend them. Even then, *never* think about technique when you are playing golf.

How to practice and learn

The best way to learn the golf swing and golf itself is from the hole back. Start on the putting green. Begin with very short putts, then move back to longer ones. You can learn almost everything you need to know about the swing by doing this. The putting stroke is pendulum-like, back and through with very little independent movement of the hands. As the swing gets longer, the hands will cock and uncock naturally and the body will begin to turn back and through. But the basic swing is the same.

Move from putting to chipping, the little shots from the edge of the green with a more lofted club. Then move back a few yards to the pitch shot with an even more lofted club and a longer swing, getting the ball more in the air so it doesn't roll so far after landing. As you do this, you'll be developing a feel that will carry over to the full swing.

As I mentioned in Chapter 3, this is practice that you can do at home, in your living room and your back yard.

Take your time. Don't expect an instant golf swing. Go slow and get it right. Your improvement will be faster.

When you have graduated to the full swing, don't forget the short game in your practice sessions. I'm amazed at the number of golfers I see on the practice tee who spend most of their time bashing shots with the driver. Less than 40 percent of the shots you will make in a round of golf will be with full swings. More than 60 percent will be short-game shots, the shots that can save you strokes and that are fun to play. Anybody, no matter how much or little strength he or she has, can learn to play them well.

So practice them. If you're going to be hitting them 60 percent of the time, spend 60 percent of your practice time on them. Take Tom Kite's advice—play games with yourself or with others. Have fun playing practice.

A word of advice—hitting practice shots *is* a lot of fun for many players, but don't hit them indiscriminately. If you beat so many balls that you get tired, your practice becomes counterproductive. Try for quality, not quantity. Once you have hit two or three good shots with one club, move on to another. When you have hit a couple of good shots with every club you want to practice, quit for the day. Then you'll be eager to come back the next time.

How to get the most out of a teacher

You don't need formal instruction to have fun playing golf, or even to get better at it. You can have fun for the rest of your life with no more instruction than I've given you in this chapter. But on the off chance that you *really* want to be as good as you can be (and I'll bet on that, because most of us do), it might be wise to seek the help of a competent and compatible teacher. This holds for beginners and players at any level.

The operative word here is *compatible*. You must find an instructor who is willing to work with you in achieving your goals. I know, maybe you're not sure right now what your goals are. I hope your first one is to develop a simple, repeating swing based on a model, as I discussed earlier. As you progress, your goals might change, but for right now that's enough.

For example, the teacher who transformed Nick Faldo into one of the top golfers in the world is not the teacher you want. Nick's goals are different than yours at the moment. He's trying to win major championships. You just want to have fun playing golf.

How to find a teacher? The referral method is good for starters. Seek out some friends who have taken lessons and ask who they recommend. Talk to as many golfers as possible. Reputations are made by word-of-mouth. There may be a teacher in your area who is particularly good with beginners. And don't forget that, even though you don't belong to a club, most private club professionals can and will take on outside pupils.

When you find one who sounds good, call that teacher and ask some questions. Find out if he or she is willing to deal with you at your level. Ask about credentials. Most competent instructors are members of the Professional Golfers Association (PGA) of America or the Teaching and Club Professional Division of the Ladies Professional Golfers Association (LPGA), although there are exceptions.

Once you start taking a lesson, tell the teacher what you want and make sure you are getting it. Don't let the professional confuse you.

If you don't understand what is meant, stop and ask and get it clarified. You'll have to learn the language so you don't have conflicting thoughts running through your mind. And don't let the pro give you more than you can handle at one time. Three different thoughts are about all that can be assimilated in one lesson.

If the teacher doesn't suggest some drills for you to do, ask about them. They are excellent aids to learning the parts of the swing and blending them into a whole. Once you begin to get the feeling of your swing, there are manuals and books available that offer effective drills in specific areas.

Ask your teacher to give you playing lessons. It's on the course where you really learn to play golf instead of just swinging a club. A good teacher will be happy to do that. It will help you improve more quickly.

And make sure your personalities mesh. If the chemistry isn't right, if learning and practice becomes work rather than fun and the process starts to get intimidating, find another teacher.

Teachers are valuable not only for their instruction but because another set of eyes can see you as you really are. Even the great players have teachers, because they can't see themselves and might not be doing what they think they're doing with their swings.

The video camera has been a boon to learning. If your professional doesn't videotape your lesson, you might want to do it yourself. That way you can match feelings with what you see on tape and can better refine your own model. That lets you practice more effectively when the teacher isn't there.

The cost of lessons will vary depending on where you live and who you go to, but the national average is about $25 for 30 minutes. I'd recommend, however, that you sign up for a full hour in the beginning, because that gives both you and the professional more time to determine your swing goals and how to achieve them.

Other learning sources

Golf magazines. Instruction books. Instruction videos. Golf schools. They are readily available, and all can help you learn. But be careful. Articles and books can help you with preswing fundamentals. That's good. They can give you the different positions in the swing. That's maybe not so good. Until you are capable enough, and have enough time, to refine the nuances of your swing, positions are not what you should be concerned about. The feeling of your swing as patterned after your swing model is what you want.

Videos, if they happen to be by a teacher or player with your swing characteristics, can help you see the swing and copy it. But you still have to internalize your own swing and be able to feel it rather than think about it.

Books, magazines and videos can be especially valuable when they deal with how to play the game—strategy, how to think your way around a golf course, the mental and emotional factors involved. I'd encourage you to read all of that information that you can.

In all cases, avoid an information overload. Confusion is not what you want. If you can pick out points that can help you perform better, fine. If you find yourself getting in trouble and your shots aren't going where you want, go back to your model and the feel of your swing.

Golf schools? Same deal. When you think you're ready to go to one and absorb the information you'll get there, go right ahead. There are many good ones that can help *(see listing starting on page 95).* Use the referral method if you can. Talk to folks who have been. Before you commit, call and ask how the school's instructors teach—will they give you a methodology or work with your needs? The good ones will do the latter. Then hold them to it. Find out how much time will be devoted to the short game and on-course play. These may be the most important things you can learn at a golf school or anywhere else.

How to learn to play

I can hear you saying it. "Whoa, do I have to go through all this before I get to play golf?" The answer is a definite "not". You can play golf any time you want. Learning the golf swing and playing golf are different, remember?

You learn to swing by playing practice. You learn to play golf by playing golf. There is no other way, nor would you want there to be. *Playing* golf is what it's all about.

Just don't practice your golf swing while you're playing golf. Don't think about technique. Let your instincts, your intelligence, take over and do what your body and mind are capable of doing.

Play safely, courteously and quickly. That's all the golf course operator cares about. That's all your playing companions and the players behind you care about. That's all you should care about, whether you're a beginner or a tour professional. You know how to do that. If you're a beginner or a player at any level, you don't have to finish every hole, sink every putt. If things aren't going well at the moment, pick up the ball and go to the next tee. Score is not important unless you're playing in a tournament.

Hit the ball, find it and hit it again. Enjoy the good shots and don't despair over the bad ones. Learn from both. Enjoy the fresh air, the green grass and your companions. Enjoy the *game*. The only reason you're playing golf is to have fun.

Several years ago I was playing in Northern Ireland at Royal Portrush, one of the greatest, most beautiful and most difficult courses in the world, with Sean Belford, then the executive director of the Northern Ireland Tourist Board. We had been joined by an American who was a visiting professor at Dublin University. He had taken the train from Dublin, some three hours away, to play Portrush. He was a pleasant companion although not particularly skilled, and he was having trouble with the thick rough. He must have lost a dozen balls but he never complained, searching quickly, then simply dropping another and playing on.

As Sean and I walked together down the final hole, I remarked that there are some people who should not play Portrush and our friend unfortunately was one of them.

Later, over sandwiches and stout in the clubhouse, the professor announced that he was spending the night in Portrush and would return to play the course the next day. And suddenly I realized I was wrong—he *should* play Portrush. The lost balls and the many strokes were of no account. He had fun, and he was coming back for more fun.

So, I reckon, will you....and I hope you do it for the rest of your life.   ∎

Other Publications

If you would like to know more about what's covered in this chapter, here is some additional suggested reading.

How to Become a Complete Golfer (Bob Toski and Jim Flick, Hardcover, Published 1990 by Golf Digest)

Learning Golf: The How-To-Learn Book for Aspiring Golfers (Chuck Hogan, Paperback, Published 1993 by Sports Production Associates)

Golf Lessons (National Golf Foundation, Paperback, Published 1985 by National Golf Foundation)

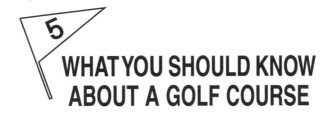

WHAT YOU SHOULD KNOW ABOUT A GOLF COURSE

G olf courses may be the most beautiful playing fields in all of
sport. They come in an infinite variety of lengths and looks.
Not one is alike, which is one of the aspects that makes golf
so much fun. Yet they are well-defined playing fields, and each has
characteristics common to all the others.

The overall course

A golf course usually is made up of eighteen holes. These are
divided into sets of nine that are known as the first and second nines
or front and back nines. Some courses have only nine holes, so if you
want to play an 18-hole round, you play the nine twice.

Each hole within a course has been assigned a *par*, which is the
score an expert should make with errorless play and two strokes on
the putting surface. A par-3 hole would require one good shot to reach
the green, a par-4 two shots and a par-5 three shots.

The United States Golf Association, the ruling body of golf in this
country, offers yardages as a guide to setting par. For men, a par-3
is up to 250 yards long, a par-4, is from 251 to 470 and a par-5, is
471 and longer. For women, a par-3 can measure up to 210 yards,
a par-4 from 211 to 400, a par-5 from 401 to 575 and a par-6 from
576 and beyond. These yardages are not arbitrary. Configuration of
the ground, hazards and other unusual conditions should be considered.

The standard mix of holes is four par-3s, four par-5s and 10 par-
4s for a total par of 72. But many courses vary from this. There are

great golf courses with pars of 69 and 70, and a par of 73 or 74 is not uncommon in Great Britain and other parts of Europe.

Par really means very little. In stroke play (also called medal play), you add up your scores on each hole and that's what you shot. Match play is hole-by-hole competition where par doesn't matter. It's simply a standard against which you can measure yourself. Its primary value is helping the television folks keep track of tournament leaders—"Lee Trevino finished at four under...." You rarely hear them say he shot 68.

The total length of a course can vary from 5,000 yards or so to more than 7,000, depending on which set of tees are used (I'll get to that in a moment). Some courses stretch much longer than 7,000 yards from the back tees (avoid those unless you're Godzilla), and there are some wonderful and challenging courses that measure no more than 6,000 to 6,500.

The tee or teeing ground

Play on each hole starts from here. A tee is a closely mown area that can be any shape or size. The actual teeing area is defined by two "tee markers" set several yards apart. The ball may be teed up on a wooden tee. It must be played from between the tee markers and up to two club-lengths behind them.

Each hole usually has three or more sets of tees, differentiated by color. This is to let you play the course at a length best suited to your strength and skill. The forward tee markers are usually red, the middle markers white and the back markers blue. Sometimes there are gold or "championship" markers farther back. Beginning golfers should play from the foward tees.

The approximate length the course measures from each set of tees is indicated on the scorecard. Once you choose a set of tees, you usually play from the same set throughout the round, although that's not mandatory in casual play. Sometimes it's fun to skip around (and sometimes it's prudent, especially if a long carry over water looms).

Fairway

It's not hard to see how this part of the course got its name. It's the closely mown area between the teeing ground and the green, and it's certainly the best route to get from one to the other. Keep it on the short grass as much as you can. The game is a lot easier from there. A fairway that bends to the right or left is called a *dogleg*.

Yardage markers indicate the distance to the green. Usually set at or near the edges of fairways, they are sometimes as subtle as a bush or as prominent as a stake.

Rough

This is the grass usually bordering each side of a fairway that is not so closely mown. Rough can vary from four inches or so in the U.S. Open (which you probably won't be worrying about for a while) to a couple of inches on most courses. Many courses have a "first cut" of rough a few feet wide that is cut at somewhere between fairway and rough height, usually an inch or inch and a half.

Your ball can get entangled in rough of any consequence and you usually can't hit shots from it as far as normal. As tour star Hubert Green once said, "That's why they call it 'rough.' If it were easy they'd call it 'easy.' "

Out of bounds

These are areas bordering the golf course on which play is prohibited. Usually they are defined by white stakes, sometimes by fences or walls. Chapter 6 will explain how to proceed if you hit your ball out of bounds.

Bunkers

Commonly known as sand traps, these are hazards that are depressions filled with sand. There are fairway bunkers that line the fairway some distance from the green, or greenside bunkers placed next to the putting surface. Greenside bunkers are more difficult to play from, although not as difficult as most of us imagine them to be.

Legend has it that the first bunkers were formed in Scotland by sheep burrowing to seek warmth from the wind, then were filled with sand blowing from the beach.

Water hazards

By definition, a water hazard is "any sea, lake, pond, river, ditch, surface drainage ditch or other open water course." It doesn't have to contain water, but it should be marked by yellow stakes or lines. Usually they are impossible and at best difficult to play from. If you can't play the ball, you have to take a penalty stroke and drop behind the point where your ball entered the hazard.

A *lateral water hazard* is a hazard or part of one that usually sits to the side or parallel to the line of play so that you can't drop behind it. It's defined by red stakes or lines. We'll deal further with how to handle these situations in the chapter on rules.

Yardage marker

This is a marker that indicates the distance to the green. It can be a distinctive tree, a bush or a stake, usually set at or near the edge of

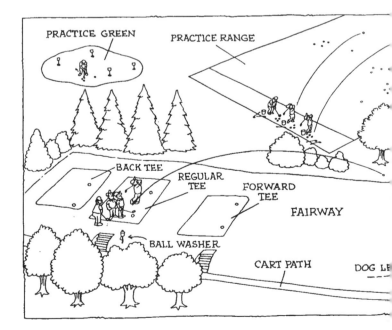

the fairway. Markers of this type almost always indicate 150 yards to the green. Some courses have plates set in the middle of the fairway. Some have three on each hole: blue indicating 200 yards to the green, white indicating 150 and red indicating 100. And it's becoming increasingly common to mark various sprinkler heads in the fairway with the yardages. In virtually all cases, the yardages are to the *middle* of the green.

Hole

This is your destination, the place you want your ball to end up after the fewest possible number of strokes. It's a circular hole, 4 1/4 inches in diameter and at least four inches deep, cut into the green. It's also called a cup.

Flagstick

Also called a "pin," it's a rod placed in the hole to show its location on the green (those little holes are hard to see from a couple hundred yards away). The flagstick usually has a flag or some other indicator attached at the top. Sometimes there is a colored plastic ball attached at varying heights to show whether the hole is located in the front, middle or back of the green.

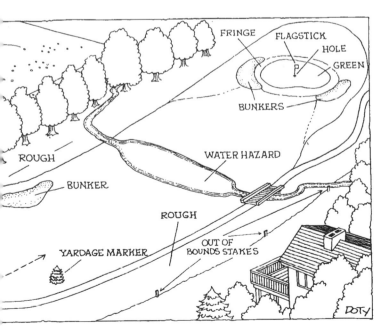

Green

This is the area in which the hole is located. It has the shortest grass on the course so you can putt or roll the ball smoothly. A green can be any size and shape, with any amount of slope and undulation. On the green is where you can save more strokes than any place else on the course. Make the green your friend.

Fringe

Also called an apron or collar, this is an area usually about 18 inches wide that encircles the putting surface. It is mowed shorter than the surrounding fairway or rough but slightly longer than the green itself.

Practice areas

Usually located adjacent to the clubhouse and course, these are areas used for practicing and improving your swing and for warming up before a round. Both options are recommended. There are usually markers to show you where you may hit from. Practice balls can be purchased either from the golf shop or the bag room or from coin- or token-operated machines at the range. You can inquire at the shop. Many practice areas now include target greens for short- and long-swing practice, as well as bunkers and practice greens for working on your short game. Almost always there is a putting green to work on that most important part of your game.

Practice or warm up, then go to the course for some fun. ■

Other Publications

If you would like to know more about what's covered in this chapter, here is some additional suggested reading.

Golf Architecture (Alistair MacKenzie, Hardcover, Published 1997 by Storey Communications)

HOW GOLF COURSES OPERATE

There are three basic types of golf facilities: *public, resort, and private.*

A public facility is just that—it's open to the public on a pay-as-you-go or sometimes a season-ticket basis. Pay your money and get your tee time. The course or courses may be owned by a municipality or county, in which case residents usually get a break on the fee and on tee times. Or it may be a privately owned course that caters to public play. Sometimes these are known as "daily fee" or "semi-private" courses, and often you can buy "memberships" that will allow you to play for an annual fee. Or you can just pay by the round. There are over 2,360 municipal and nearly 8,000 daily fee courses in the U.S.

As the term implies, a resort course is affiliated with a resort and is always available to resort guests. In most cases it also is open to anyone not staying at the resort, normally at a higher fee.

A private club is open only to members and their guests. In some cases, guests are required to play with a member. At other clubs, a member's recommendation is enough to get guests on the course. In any event, you have to know someone who belongs. There's about 4,200 private golf facilities in the U.S. today.

Many courses today are being built in connection with real estate communities. Some are open to the public, but most are available only to property owners in the development. Often there is an extra fee to join the club. Some of these courses are open to the public when first built and become private as lot and home sales increase.

You'll soon get to know which courses are available to you in your area, but if you travel and like to play on the road, here's a hint—many courses open to the public bill themselves as "country clubs" or "golf clubs." If you're not sure, a phone call will tell you.

So you have to find a place to play and figure out how to do it. If you have some friends with experience in the game, they can guide you. As noted earlier, a good golf professional will be happy to help. Barring those options, let's take a look at some things here.

Getting a tee time

First you have to get a tee time. Most public courses are listed in the Yellow Pages. Make a phone call and determine what the procedure is at the course you want to play. Most courses accept reservations by phone, although usually they must be made in advance. That's especially true for weekend play. In some of the more crowded metropolitan areas, getting a weekend reservation demands that you arrive early in the morning and wait in line. That's something you should find out. It's often possible, especially during the week, to walk up and get a tee time, but it's best to call ahead.

If you're alone, be sure to explain that you'd like to be paired with a group. That shouldn't be a problem, even on weekends. Golf is usually played in groups of four, or foursomes, and there often are single openings into which they can fit you. It's probably easier for a single to find a game than it is for two players. You may have to get there early on the weekend and maybe wait until an opening comes up, but you can practice your putting until it does.

Even if you're a beginning or inexperienced player, don't be intimidated by playing with strangers. Remember, you can play safely, courteously and quickly with the best of them. The worst thing that can happen is that you may make some new friends.

Price to play varies

You have to pay. Nothing is free. But public golf, relative to everything else, is still affordable. Yes, Pebble Beach, site of three U.S. Opens and the annual AT&T Invitational, is a public course and you can play there for only $305. Well, that *does* includes a golf car. If you stay at The Lodge at Pebble Beach, golf will cost you only $245. Room rates start at $350 a night.

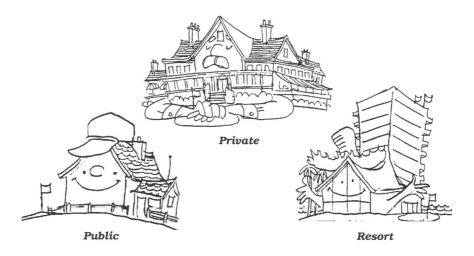

Private

Public

Resort

The overall accessibility of golf is reflected in the fact that nearly 70% of the more than 14,500 golf courses in the U.S. today are open to the public.

But if you just want to go down the street for a round, the national average for green fees at semi-private courses for weekday and weekend play is about $21 and $25; at municipal courses, for residents, it's $17 and $19. Juniors and seniors often get a discount. Most courses sell season tickets that can save you money if you play regularly. Green fees will vary with locale and with how closely a course operator thinks his layout approximates Pebble Beach, but for the most part golf is still cheaper than skiing and some other pastimes.

To get the resident rate at most municipal and county courses, you may have to get an identification card. Ask at the course about how to do it.

Golf car fees at municipal and semi-private courses average $15 and $17 a round for two persons. You usually can carry your own bag if you want, and if you don't have a physical disability you should. You'll end up in better shape and you'll enjoy the game more. Many courses still rent pull-carts or trolleys for a nominal fee, or you can buy your own for around $50. Caddies, unfortunately, are rare at public facilities these days, especially those who depend on golf car rentals for a large share of their revenue. If they are available and you want one, ask at the golf shop desk what the fees are. They probably will run a little higher than the golf car cost. And don't forget to add a tip if the caddie does a good job.

Getting to know who's who

There are personnel you should know about. Every facility has a head professional or director of golf who is in charge of the day-to-day golf operation. He or she may have one or more assistant professionals. There may be teaching professionals from whom you can take lessons (don't forget the guidelines in Chapter 4). If the operation is a large one, there will be shop assistants who collect your green fee and will help you purchase merchandise.

There may be a bag drop at the course you're playing. If so, unload your clubs there and an attendant should put them on a golf car if you wish. At the larger operations, there may be an attendant who cleans your clubs and takes them to the bag rack after your round. In this case, it's good form to tip a dollar or two.

Most public facilities have starters who make sure everybody gets off the first tee on time. Some even handle the reservations, so you'll have to find out how it works at your course. Again, a phone call should do it.

On the course you're likely to see somebody riding around in a cart marked "ranger." He's there to see that play moves quickly and smoothly. If your group is falling behind, he may warn you to pick up the pace. But of course that won't happen to you.

Behind the scenes is the golf course superintendent, who is in charge of a crew that mows the grass, maintains the bunkers and performs all the other operations that keep the course in good condition. You may encounter mowers and the like at certain times. Usually the operators will stop while your group plays through, but don't automatically count on it.

Most course have other facilities that include a snack bar and/or dining area and a cocktail lounge or at least a bar. There also may be a "halfway house" on the course where you can stop for a drink or a snack. Many courses have locker rooms where you can change your shoes, although it's not considered bad form to change them in the parking lot.

Some hints about golf vacations

In case you want to play vacation golf at some point or are involved in a business convention, a resort operation is structured basically the same as a public course, with only a few differences. A bellhop usually can take your clubs from the car and have them stored in the bag room if you wish. If your tee times have not already been

Every round of golf begins in the pro shop where you sign in, pay your fees and have a chance to check out the latest in equipment and apparel.

arranged, you can call the starter or the reservations desk from your room to do so. Golf cars are mandatory at almost all resorts. And the cost of both car and green fees generally will be higher than at a semi-private or municipal course. It's wise to find out the golf fees before you go, just as you might also check out the room fees.

If you are invited to play at a private club, check with your host on tipping and other policies. Generally someone will pick your bag up at your car or from the bag drop, and you should tip him a dollar or two. A similar tip should go to the locker attendant who shines your shoes. (At a private club, changing from street to golf shoes in the parking lot from the trunk of your car is considered inappropriate).

If by now you have the golf bug for real and are considering joining a private club, here are some guidelines. You usually must be sponsored by a member. Once you know one, he or she can take you through the process. Costs will vary. Usually there is an initiation fee that can range from a few thousand dollars to as much as $50,000. There are some in the United States that charge into the six figures. If that doesn't make you blink, go for it. On top of that, there will be a structure of monthly or annual dues.

If you can afford all this and are serious about it, first be sure that the course and the club facilities are compatible with your and your family's needs.

If you have a choice, that should be the criterion for any course that you play.   ■

1 EQUIPMENT—HOW AND WHAT TO BUY

G olf started out as a club and ball game. It remains so today. You can't play it without either. But choosing that club and ball has become a lot more complicated. The rules require that clubs maintain a traditional look and balls must adhere to size and weight standards, but the change in the construction of that equipment over the years has been dramatic.

The beginning golfer—or any golfer—now faces a bewildering array of choices as equipment manufacturers pursue the technological revolution. There are cast irons, forged irons, irons covered with graphite, perimeter-weighted irons, classic blades, laminated woods, persimmon woods, woods made of metal and graphite (if you can believe that), shafts of steel, graphite and titanium with a whole lot of different weights, flexes and torque points, and, grips made of rubber, leather and composite materials.

There are three-piece balls and two-piece balls, balls covered with balata and balls covered with Surlyn and other exotic materials, balls with dimple patterns that make them fly higher, lower and in between, balls

Today's players face a sometimes bewildering array of choices.

that spin a lot and balls that spin less.

Do you need to know all this? Not at the moment. The sophisticated stuff can come as your skill and enthusiasm increase. The newer golfer needs only the simplest gear that works.

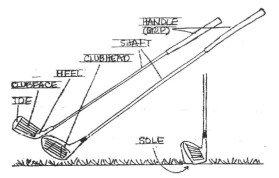

Knowing the basic components of a golf club can help your game in many ways.

You probably have figured this out, but a golf club has three parts—the head, the shaft and the handle or grip, which covers the end of the shaft so you can hold the club. A set of clubs contains *woods* and *irons* (that's what they've always been called—we'll forget about the various materials they can be made of). Woods have a broader shape, irons a thinner blade. The length of the club shafts vary; the driver having the longest, the wedges having the shortest. The loft of clubheads—the amount the clubface is tilted back

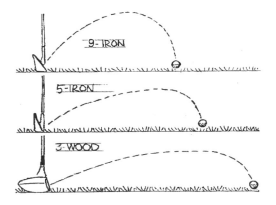

Distance and trajectory are dictated by the angle (loft) of the clubface. Golf clubs are numbered. The higher the number, the greater the loft.

from vertical—also vary, from the straight-faced driver to the high-lofted wedge. The longer the shaft and the straighter the clubface, the farther the ball will go. The more loft the club has, the higher and shorter it will hit the ball. The higher the number on the club, whether it be wood or iron, the more loft it has.

Buying a set of clubs

You can buy a complete set of clubs for less than $150. Or you can buy a single driver for $1,700. You can buy clubs from catalogs, at department stores, sporting goods stores, off-course discount stores staffed by professionals and on-course golf shops. Club-repair shops and small, independent clubmakers also are an option I'd recommend you explore. You can buy a set of used clubs at a tag sale or from the want ads. Do comparison shopping to see where you can get the best bargain.

The official rules of golf allow a maximum of 14 clubs, but you don't necessarily need that many in the beginning. Starter sets that cost less than $150 may be all you need at the moment. Usually they come with driver, 3-wood, 3-, 5-, 7- and 9-iron and putter. If you have a choice, a 3-wood, 5-wood, 4-, 6- and 8-irons, pitching wedge, sand wedge and putter might be the best combination. Later you can fill in or trade up to a complete set.

Trading up can be important. Some professionals will be willing to sell you a starter set, then give you the value back on a new and better set as your skill increases and your needs change. See if you can find one who will do that.

Making sure your clubs fit you

There's a proviso to all of this. No matter what kind or quality of clubs you buy, *it's important that they fit.* It's okay to play with borrowed or rented clubs when you're trying to decide if you like the game. Once you do, find clubs that will match your build and your swing. Ill-fitting clubs can hinder your development.

What fits? *Weight, length, lie angle at impact* and *shaft flex,* as well as *grip size,* are the critical factors. Your clubs should not be so heavy that you can't handle them nor so light that you can't feel them when you swing. Length and lie angle, which is the angle between the ground and the shaft when the club is properly soled or placed, are linked together. If your clubs

Making sure your clubs have the proper "lie angle" can make a difference.

are too long, the lie probably will be too upright, the toe of the club pointing too much in the air. If they're too short, the lie will be too flat, the heel of the club off the ground at address. This will adversely affect the direction of your shots.

The size of the grip or handle is important. When you hold the club with normal pressure in your target-side hand (left for righthanders, right for lefties), the tips of your index and ring fingers should barely touch the pad under your thumb. If the grip is too small or too big, your control of the club and the direction your ball flies will be affected.

As you progress in the game, it's critical that you be fitted with the correct shaft. The shaft bends backward and forward and downward and also twists or torques during the swing, depending on its firmness and how fast you swing it. That affects the lie angle at impact and the control and distance of your shots. Generally, the slower you swing the more flexible the shaft should be, and vice versa. But because most golfers can't accurately determine their swing speeds, it's important that you get help from a professional when buying. That eliminates any outlet that can't give it to you.

If you're taking lessons, buy there. Tell the pro what you can afford. They will usually work within that range to fit you. If not, go elsewhere.

About golf balls

Golf balls? For now, make sure they have Surlyn or other cutproof covers. It says on the box, or the shop clerk can help you. Balata balls that the pros and better amateurs use have softer covers that cut easily when mis-hit. Frankly, you're going to mis-hit some. We all do. Balls cost from $10 to as high as $50 a dozen, depending on where you buy them, so durable balls can save you money. Trajectory and spin characteristics can wait until you get further into the game, although many of the newer durable balls perform comparably to balata in those areas. When you're starting out, good used balls often available in professional shops will work as well as new ones and are a lot less expensive.

Bags and shoes

You'll need a few other things. A lightweight bag for your clubs, with a couple of pockets for extra balls and rain gear, will do just fine. Golf shoes, either with spikes or composition soles with tiny cleats, will help maintain your stability and balance when you swing. They are recommended but not essential. Rubber-soled shoes or sneak-

ers will do. But shoes with slick soles or running shoes with big rubber cleats are not appropriate.

You might want a golf glove to help keep your left or target hand from slipping as you swing, but some good players do without one. You'll need some wooden tees, which you can buy in the golf shop, a ball marker (a coin will do) and a small tool for repairing ball marks on the green, which most shops give away. Other than that, carry the usual outdoor accessories—a cap or visor, rainsuit or windbreaker, umbrella, hand towel and some sunscreen.

That's all you need. Now go have some fun. ■

Other Publications

If you would like to know more about what's covered in this chapter, here is some additional suggested reading.

The Insider's Guide to Golf Equipment: The Fully Illustrated, Comprehensive Directory of Brand-Name Clubs and Accessories (Nick Mastroni, Paperback, Published 1997 by Perizes)

Special Equipment Issues of *GOLF* and *Golf Digest* magazines

HOW TO PLAY SAFELY,
COURTEOUSLY AND QUICKLY

J ust follow the Golden Rule—do unto others as you would have them do unto you. Safely, courteously, quickly. That's what etiquette is all about on a golf course, as it is almost everywhere else in life. Being considerate of other golfers and the environment will cover most of the situations during a round.

Let's look at the categories:

How to play quickly

Golf is not a race. Neither should it be a death march. It can be played quickly and comfortably just by observing a few simple rules.

First, be aware of your pace of play. Assess your shot and choose your club while others are hitting. When it's your turn, hit the ball and go find it as quickly as possible, whether you're walking or riding in a golf car. Walking quickly is better exercise anyway.

The Rules of Golf say that the golfer who is away, or farthest from the hole, should play first. But "ready golf" is more practical and speedier in informal play. That simply means that you play when you're ready, even if you're not away. Just make sure nobody is in the line of fire.

If you hit your ball into the rough or the trees, watch carefully where it goes and mark the spot with a reference point so you don't have to spend a lot of time looking for it. If you think it can't be found or is out of bounds, play a provisional ball (that will be covered in the next chapter).

On the green, line up your putt while others are putting (but don't bother other players while you're doing it). If you're closest to the hole, you tend the flagstick. If you're the last to hole out, you put the flagstick back. Then you and everybody in the group should leave the green quickly—no practice putts, please, and mark your score on the next tee while others are hitting.

If you're riding in a golf car with another player, drop your mate off at his or her ball, then drive to your own and get ready for your shot.

If you're riding at a course that doesn't allow cars off the paths, park the car adjacent to the ball and take several clubs so you don't have to walk back in case your first guess was wrong. Do the same thing around the green if your ball has missed the putting surface. If you're walking, of course, none of this is a problem.

Whenever possible, drop your bag or park your golf car in line with the next tee, so you don't have to retrace your steps.

Four players should finish an 18-hole round of golf in four hours or less under normal circumstances. Don't be influenced by the five-hour tournament rounds you see on television. Many of those folks are in another zone.

So you're a beginner and are taking a lot of strokes, which takes more time. That may happen for awhile. It does for everybody. So if the group behind is looming closer, pick up the ball and go to the next tee. Remember? Score is not important at the moment. Having fun is. If it's going badly, forget it and let yourself do better on the next hole. You'll be amazed at how things can turn around.

How to play safely

Don't hurt anybody, including yourself. Simple enough.

Stand clear of others when you're taking a practice swing. Make sure nobody is standing nearby or in front of you when you hit your shot. And make sure you avoid the same sin. Walking ahead too close to another player's line of shot can be dangerous to your health. Golf balls can hurt.

Wait to hit until players ahead of you are out of reach. This goes for maintenance workers, too. If it's a blind shot, somebody should go ahead to check.

If you have a trouble shot, as from the woods, warn other players that the ball could ricochet. And move out of range if somebody else is trying it.

Being considerate of your fellow players and the environment are prerequisites to enjoying the game.

If you hit a wild shot toward another group of players (yes, it sometimes happens), yell "Fore" as loudly as possible. That's because if you shout, "Look out, Bill," the ball may be there by the third syllable. "Fore" is the universal warning.

Drive golf cars carefully and with your feet inside. Legs dangling outside have been broken. And don't drive up and down the sides of steep slopes, or too fast on any slope. Lives have been lost that way. Drive as if it's an automobile (and not at the Indy 500).

Throwing or banging clubs is a no-no. It can be dangerous to your health and to the person around you. But then, why would you want to throw a club anyway? This is only a game!

If lightning is in the area—anywhere—get off the course as quickly as possible. If the clubhouse is too far, find cover in a shelter, or in low-lying areas or bunkers and away from water. Don't ever mess with that stuff.

Watch out for poisonous plants, bees and ticks; especially if you're wearing shorts. And, of course, protect your skin from the sun (almost everything is bad for us anymore, isn't it?).

How to play courteously

Be considerate of others. That's all you have to remember. Golf is a game for ladies and gentlemen, people who care about other people. Being nice doesn't make the game any less fun, and it also will get you quickly accepted by other players. Rude folks find themselves looking fruitlessly for a game. Solitaire may be their best answer.

Stand clear of others while they are playing a shot. Several yards to the ball side, not in back of them and *never* in front of them is a good rule.

Be careful when you talk. You're not attending a wake. You can talk, tell jokes, laugh and whoop it up on a golf course. That's part of the fun and companionship. Just don't do it when a fellow player is trying to make a six-foot putt. It's like the phone ringing during a tender moment. Ruins the effect.

And please don't complain about your bad shots or babble on about what's wrong with your swing and what you need to do about it. As I mentioned earlier, nobody cares. Your playing companions will congratulate you on a good shot, as you should theirs, and say nothing about a bad one. Your opponents probably secretly hope you'll hit another bad one, and your partner hopes you'll rectify the problem before the next shot. He or she is not really interested in how you're going to do it.

Be aware of others on the course. If your group is looking for a lost ball or is otherwise playing slowly and holding up the players behind more than momentarily, wave them through. Stand aside while they do so, then make an effort to play more swiftly.

Take care of the course. On a shot from the fairway or rough you're likely to take out a piece of turf, called a divot. Replace it as best you can in its original position and press it down with your foot. The

When looking for a lost ball, a common courtesy is to allow the group behind you to play through.

grass will grow again. If you're playing on Bermuda grass, there often will be containers of soil on your golf car. Fill in the hole you created with this. Do the same with soil often provided on tees.

When your ball lands on the green it will create a ball mark or pitch mark. Repair it with the small tool you can find in golf shops. Lift the outer edges of the crater inward and up, then tap down with your putter. A repaired ball mark heals quickly. One not repaired takes weeks.

Replace divots and repair ball marks other than your own. Be nicer than the thoughtless players.

A ball mark improperly repaired takes weeks to heal.

Enter a bunker from the low side, not the high side. When you're finished with your shot, carefully use the rake provided to smooth out your footprints and the crater you made in the sand. Leave a nice playing surface for the golfers behind you.

Avoid stepping in another player's line on the putting surface. This makes indentations that can throw a ball off line. And it can make spike marks in the green. The rules say you can repair old ball marks in your line but you cannot tap down spike marks. Some don't agree with this rule, but there it is. In any event, you can help by tapping down spike marks around the cup *after* you putt. It's just another courtesy to other players.

Be careful around the cup in removing and replacing the flagstick and in retrieving your

Repairing ball marks and raking footprints out of bunkers are high on the list of golf etiquette.

ball. Take your ball out with your hand, not with your club, a silly maneuver that seems to be in favor with some. Avoid breaking down the edges.

Don't drive golf cars too close to the green and certainly not on the green or through bunkers. Or don't drop your bag of clubs on the green.

Put your paper cups and candy wrappers in the trash containers, not on the ground. You wouldn't litter your front lawn, would you?

Leave the course as you found it....or better, if you can.

That's not a bad idea for the planet, is it?   ∎

Other Publications

If you would like to know more about what's covered in this chapter, here is some additional suggested reading.

Golf Etiquette (Barbara Puett and Jim Apfelbaum, Hardcover, Published 1992, St. Martins Press)

9
THE RULES OF THE GAME

Rules ... boy, do we have rules! But don't get nervous. This can be simple.

In the beginning there were just 13 rules of golf, drawn up in 1744 by the Honourable Company of Edinburgh Golfers in Scotland, the first organized golf society. The code was adopted almost word for word by the Royal and Ancient Golf Club of St. Andrews when it drew up its own "original" rules in 1754. The articles were revised in 1755 and again in 1809, and these three sets of laws form the foundation of the rules we know today.

Now, however, there are 34 rules, most of them quite lengthy, plus a section on etiquette, a section on definitions, four long appendices, a set of rules of amateur status and a book of decisions on the rules that runs well more than 500 pages. Whew!

Do you have to memorize all this? No, never. Should you be familiar with the rules, so you know where to look in the book when a situation arises? Probably, at some point. When you start playing with others for money, marbles or drinks, you'll want to play by the rules as much as possible because they will be. If you play in a tournament, an acquaintance with the rules is even more helpful.

Golf is about fun. It's also about honor and sportsmanship. And it's about the challenge to do your best, whether it be on a single shot, a hole or a round. Meeting that challenge brings the self-satisfaction, which breeds the fun. Meeting that challenge within the rules is what makes the game so fascinating. Attaining a goal by violating the rules doesn't satisfy anybody.

Right now, however, you're just trying to have fun learning the game, so don't clutter your head with a lot of legislation. There are just a few basic rules you need to know to get around the course. In fact, at the risk of offending the purists. I'm going to suggest that you bend a few of them for the time being.

One of the basic prcccpts of thc game is that you play the ball as it lies at all times (you are allowed to mark and replace your ball on the putting surface). But you might want to play "winter rules" or "preferred lies" for awhile. Learning to hit the ball solidly is tough enough without trying to hit it out of a divot or a scruffy lie. Move it to a nice patch of grass and swing at it. If it's buried in the rough and you can't hope to get it out, move it to a better place. Throw it out in the fairway for all anybody cares. Make it as easy as possible on yourself until you can hit the ball with reasonable consistency. Score is not important at the moment. When it becomes important, to you or your companions, then start playing the ball as it lies.

Incidentally, learn to hit from bad lies and rough in practice so you can cope with them on the course. And you'll want to start playing the real game as quickly as possible, because it will make you a better player. Besides, the fun of a good shot from a bad lie is even greater than if the ball were sitting up nicely.

That said, let's look at what you need to know:

The ball

Rule 1 tells us, "The Game of Golf consists in playing a ball from the *teeing ground* into the hole by a *stroke* or successive strokes in accordance with the Rules." That's pretty easy. However, playing a ball means playing *one* ball. You're not supposed to substitute another during the play of a hole. However, if you're facing a long carry over water and want to put down an old, scuffed ball in place of your shiny, new and expensive one, nobody will tell. For now, that is.

The stroke

A stroke is the forward movement of the club made with the intention of striking the ball. Intention is the key word here. If you voluntarily stop your forward stroke halfway down, it's not a stroke, because your intention died. If you go through with the swing, it's a stroke, even if you miss the ball. There is no penalty if a ball falls or is nudged off a tee before the forward stroke begins. Also, you can't

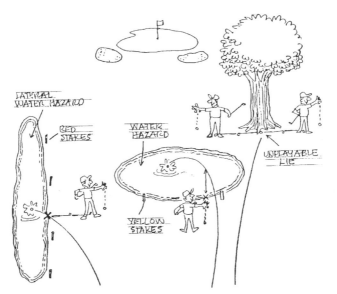

*The color of the stakes will tell you what kind of hazard you've encountered
... and where you are permitted to "drop" your ball for your next shot.*

push, scrape or "spoon" the ball. There has to be a backswing, no
matter how short, and a forward swing.

The honor

The player who had the lowest score on the previous hole has the
"honor" and is entitled to play first on the next tee. The rules say this
has to happen, but if this player stops to tie a shoestring or otherwise
dawdles, somebody else should step up and hit it. It simply saves time
and nobody cares. That's if you're not in a tournament, of course.

Hazards

Hazards are just that. They can be hazardous to your score. They
also may swallow your golf ball. There are technically two and
actually three kinds of hazards. Following is the list and how to deal
with them.

Water hazard—As explained in Chapter 5, this is any body of
water or ditch (even if there is no water in it) marked by yellow lines
or stakes. Everything within those boundaries is the hazard. A water
hazard also includes a *lateral water hazard*, which is marked by red
lines or stakes. This can get a little confusing, but hang in there. A

water hazard is a lake, pond, river, stream or whatever that lies in your path to the green. You have to hit your ball over it. If you don't do that, God forbid, and your ball drowns, you must drop a ball behind the point where it last crossed the margin of the hazard, keeping that point between the hole and where you drop the ball. You can drop as far back as you want, providing you follow that provision. And, unfortunately, you have to add a penalty stroke to your score.

A lateral water hazard (the red line or stakes, remember) is one that generally runs parallel to the hole. You can't drop *behind* it, so you must drop within two club-lengths outside the point where the ball last crossed the hazard line. Or you can drop in the same way on the opposite side of the hazard, as long as it's the same distance from the hole. Again, tack on that extra stroke if you're keeping score.

If your ball ends up within the confines of a hazard but not in the water and you can play it, make sure you don't ground your club, which means letting it rest on the surface. That's a no-no and costs you a penalty stroke. Touching the grass but not the ground is okay.

Bunker—As you already know, this is a sand trap. You don't have to drop out of it and take a penalty, but you have to play out of it. The basic rule here is that, as in a water hazard, you can't touch the sand with your club before you make the stroke.

Out of bounds

You read in Chapter 5 that out-of-bounds areas usually are defined by white stakes, sometimes by a line on the ground and sometimes by a fence or wall. The stakes and lines are out of bounds. The entire ball must lie out of bounds. If any part of it is in bounds, you can play it if possible. But you can't remove the stakes (or dismantle the fence or wall) if they interfere with your swing. You can, however, stand out of bounds to play a ball that is in bounds.

If your ball goes out of bounds, you must count the stroke and replay the shot, adding a penalty stroke. This is called the *stroke-and-distance* penalty. You count the stroke, you lose the distance and add another stroke. In other words, go back to where you hit the original shot and do it again. In the case of a drive, you're now hitting your third shot. Obviously this can be damaging to your score, not to mention your financial health if you have a little wager going. As a beginner, and rather than going back to replay, you may want to drop and hit another ball at the point at which the first ball went out-of-bounds...and take a two-stroke penalty.

Lost ball

If you hit your ball into rough, bushes, trees or other trash and aren't sure where it is, you have no more than five minutes to look for it. If you can't find it within that time, the ball is lost and you have to replay. The rule is the same as for a shot out of bounds—count the stroke, return to the original spot, add a penalty stroke and hit it again.

Provisional ball

If you think your ball may be lost or out of bounds, you're allowed to hit a provisional ball to save you the time and effort of trekking back to hit another. If

To be out of bounds, the entire ball must be outside of the stake.

your first ball is indeed out of bounds or can't be found, play the provisional. If your first ball is found and in play, put the provisional back in your pocket.

When you hit a provisional ball, you're supposed to announce, "I'm going to play a provisional ball." If you're in a tournament and you don't do it that way, the provisional ball becomes the one in play even if you find your first ball. In informal play, nobody really cares.

Unplayable lie

Sad to say, we all sometimes hit balls into places where we can't play them—usually lodged against a tree or under a pine or imbedded in a bush. When this happens to you, you have three options. 1) You can drop within two club-lengths of the spot where the ball lay, not closer to the hole, which is the most commonly used and best option if you can get adequate relief from your predicament; 2) You can proceed under the same rule as for a ball that is lost or out of bounds, returning to the original spot and replaying; or 3) You can drop as far back as you want from the point where your ball lay, keeping that point between you and the hole. In each case you count the stroke that got you in all this trouble and add a penalty stroke.

Obstructions

This is kind of complicated. To simplify, an *obstruction* is anything artificial on the course, including roads, ball washers and irrigation control boxes. Walls, fences or stakes that define out of bounds are *not* obstructions. If an obstruction—it could be a restroom, or whatever—interferes with your stance or swing, you get relief. If it's a movable obstruction, such as a bench on a tee, you can move it. If it's not movable, you can drop your ball within one club-length, not nearer the hole, from the point that gives you relief.

Understand, you get relief from interference with your *stance* and *swing*, not from interference with your line of play. If you drop correctly and now can swing freely but the object is still blocking the line of your shot, that's tough luck. You have to play around it.

Casual water and ground under repair

You're allowed a free drop within one club-length of the nearest point of relief, not closer to the hole, from either situation. Casual water is water than doesn't belong on the course, from rain or overwatering or whatever. Even if you can't see it at first, if it bubbles up under your shoes you get relief. Ground under repair is an area that's been torn up or otherwise damaged. It will be marked with a white line. If it isn't marked, you don't get relief, no matter how bad it is.

How to drop

This is not a big deal, but there is a correct procedure for dropping the ball when the occasion arises. You stand up straight, hold the ball at shoulder height and arm's length and drop it. Not too tough. If you don't do it that way in the U.S. Open, there's a one-stroke penalty. In your group at home, probably nobody cares very much. But dropping the right way does show that you know what you're doing on a golf course.

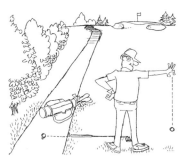

A free drop can be taken whenever your ball comes to rest on a cart path.

There's another little proviso here. If you drop a ball and it rolls closer to the hole or more than two club-lengths away, drop it again. If that happens a second time, then you're allowed to place the ball on the spot where it first touched the ground on the second drop.

On the putting green

There are a few special rules here that you should know. You can repair ball marks or old hole plugs on the putting surface, but you can't tamp down spike marks, as you know. You can't stand astride the line of the putt when you make a stroke, as in croquet.

Hitting another ball on the green with your putt can be very costly.

Watch out for other balls on the putting green. If your ball is on the green and strikes another ball on the green, you incur a two-stroke penalty in stroke play. In match play (the difference will be explained in another chapter), no penalty is incurred. If it's your ball that is hit, by the way, you must replace it without penalty. In any event, it's always a good idea for everybody to mark his or her ball with a coin when it's on the green.

If your ball is on the green and it strikes the flagstick in the hole, you are penalized two strokes in stroke play or lose the hole in match play. Either remove the flagstick or have someone attend it when you are putting.

If your ball is off the green and any of this happens, there is no penalty.

That's all you need to know about the rules for the moment. If a situation arises that you or your friends can't handle, simply do what seems fair. As you eventually get further into the rule book, you'll find that's what the rules are based on anyway. ■

Other Publications

If you would like to know more about what's covered in this chapter, here is some additional suggested reading.

Annually Updated Rules of Golf (Published by USGA, available through the National Golf Foundation)

THE HANDICAP AND SLOPE SYSTEMS

Handicap? You already have a bad back, an overabundance of advice and an overdue mortgage payment. What do you need with another handicap?

This one is different. In golf, a handicap is a number that measures your ability, or at least your current potential. You don't really need one to enjoy the game. But it's nice to have whenever you play with strangers and want to wager a few bob in a fun game, or if you want to play in a tournament.

With a handicap, you can play and bet with your friends at your home course, even if some are better and some are worse than you …just don't bet too much. At any rate, golf is now the only sport with a handicap system that allows players to compete on a near-equal basis at *any* venue.

Bowling, for example, has a handicap system based on scoring average, a player giving or receiving the commensurate number of pins depending on his or her average. But all bowling lanes are basically the same, so there is no need or method for adjusting when you are competing in different houses.

Golf is different. Each course is different, with a different degree of difficulty. In years past, handicaps often did not "travel" well because courses were incorrectly rated in comparison to others and because there was no allowance for the difference in difficulty. A 20-handicap golfer at the American Legion course in Marshalltown,

Iowa, for example, would have a tough time playing to a 20 handicap at Winged Foot, the site of several U.S. Open championships. The Legion course in Marshalltown is a very nice course, by the way, but it's not nearly as difficult as Winged Foot.

However, in the last 10 years or so, the U.S. Golf Association has implemented a Slope System in which all courses in the country are rated by the same standards and assigned a "Slope" rating designed to equalize handicaps.

Let's begin at the beginning and examine how all this works:

What a handicap does

It lets golfers of different skill levels play on an equal footing. If your handicap is 20 and you're competing at match play against a friend whose handicap is 15, you get a stroke advantage on each of the five holes designated on the scorecard (we'll get to that shortly). If he makes 5 and you make 5 on one of those holes, you win because, with your stroke, you have scored a net 4. The same holds true in four-ball, the best ball of two against the best ball of another two. If Joe is a 10 handicap, Sam is a 15, you are a 20 and Bill is a 25, you all play off of Joe's handicap. Sam gets five strokes, you get 10 and Bill gets 15 on the designated holes.

Holes are rated by difficulty from one through 18 and are so marked on the scorecard (and sometimes on a yardage marker on each tee). So you will get your strokes on the holes marked one through 10.

Men and women also can play against each other, even from different tees, using the same system and adjusting for the difference in course rating. The pro at your course can advise you how this is done.

If you are playing in a stroke or medal play event with a 20 handicap, simply add up your score at the end of the round and subtract 20 strokes. If your gross score, your real score, is 92, your net score after the handicap deduction is 72.

How you get a handicap

If you play at a public course or private club that belongs to a state or local golf association, or to the U.S. Golf Association, you can get a USGA handicap simply by signing up and paying a fee—it ranges from $6 to $15. Many public courses have a "club within a club," simply an association of golfers formed for purposes of getting a

Handicaps allow players of different skill levels to compete as equals.

handicap. Or you can form your own club with as few as ten members. All you need is a handicap committee and bylaws, and you must follow the USGA handicap system. You can get a USGA handicap index after turning in as few as five scores.

How a handicap is computed

This gets a little complicated, but you don't have to worry about it. The marvelous computer does it all for you. Just post your scores on the sheet provided or at some courses you can enter them into the computer yourself. If you really want to know how it's done, here goes: Every golf course has its own course rating and a Slope rating. Each of your last 20 adjusted gross scores must be subtracted by the course rating, then multiplied by 113 and divided by the course's Slope rating. The result number is then rounded off to the nearest tenth and is called a handicap differential.

Example:

Score	Course/Tees	Course Rating	Slope Rating
96	XYZ C.C.-white	70.6	120
98	ABC C.C.-blue	72.1	128

Handicap Differential Calculation:

$$\frac{96 - 70.6 \times 113}{120} = 23.918 \qquad \begin{array}{c} \text{Differential} \\ 23.9 \end{array}$$

$$\frac{98 - 72.1 \times 113}{128} = 22.864 \qquad 22.9$$

The ten lowest handicap differentials from your last 20 scores are then averaged and multiplied by .96 with all numbers after the tenths digit deleted resulting in your USGA handicap index.

Example:

Average of 10 lowest differentials is 22.24
22.24 x .96 = 21.350
USGA handicap index is 21.3

You will get a card that shows what scores were used, your handicap index and your home course handicap.

Oh, one more thing. You must use Equitable Stroke Control in adjusting your final score for posting purposes. That simply means you are limited as to how high your score can be on any given hole, to wit:

Course Handicap	Maximum Number on Any Hole
9 or less	6
10 through 19	7
20 through 29	8
30 through 39	9
40 or more	10

There is no limit to the number of holes on which you can adjust your score.

If you don't have a handicap and are trying to establish one, you still need to adjust your gross score before posting it. To determine the maximum number you are allowed per hole, use the index of 36.4 for men, or 40.4 for women, converted to a course handicap.

If, during a match, you are out of contention on a particular hole and pick up your ball to speed play, put down the score you most likely would have made. This need not necessarily be the highest score you are allowed.

You probably didn't want to know all that, but it's important if you want an established handicap. Incidentally, if you're playing in a tournament, you have to count all your strokes and report your real score. Then adjust that score before you post it for handicap purposes.

There are a few other nuances to the handicap system that you will learn in time, but that's enough for now. And remember, if you can't get a handicap or don't want one, golf is still just as much fun.

How the Slope System works

In a process beginning in the early 1980s, more than 11,000 courses throughout the country have been rated by teams of low- and average-handicap players trained in the rating process. Only a few hundred have not yet been rated. The teams take into consideration the length of the course and various other factors that contribute to the difficulty. They come up with both the course rating, which is based on the score a scratch golfer should shoot from a certain set of tees, and the Slope, which indicates the difficulty for the average golfer in comparison with other courses. There is a course rating and a Slope assigned to each set of tees on a course.

Pine Valley, the famed Clementon, N.J., course, and Minami outside of Honolulu, have the highest Slope ratings in the country at 152. A couple of executive courses somewhere have the lowest at 55. The standard Slope rating is 113.

How does it work? If you play at a course that has a higher Slope than the one on which you earned your handicap index, you will receive more strokes. If you play at a course with a lower Slope, you will receive fewer. Let's say your course is rated at 113 and you have a handicap index of 20.2. That translates to a home course handicap of 20. If you play at a course with a Slope of 100, your handicap there will only be 18. If the course you visit has a Slope of 125, your handicap will be 22.

How do you know? Each course will or should have handicap tables for the Slope rating posted, probably in the locker room, preferably on the first and tenth tees. The Slope for each course also will be indicated. All you have to do is note the Slope for that course and find your handicap index. That will tell you how many strokes you get there. Simple enough. Now you can play on equal footing with anybody anywhere. ∎

OTHER THINGS YOU SHOULD KNOW

G olf is a simple game, but there does seem to be a lot to know to play it comfortably and correctly. Most of this learning requires only common sense, and much of it you will pick up as you play with others. To help you get started, here's a potpourri of items large and small that will help you understand and play the game better...and enjoy it more.

How to get ready to play

To give yourself a chance to play your best, start preparing before you get to the course. If possible, allow yourself plenty of time, don't drink a lot of coffee, avoid any arguments or anything else that puts your nervous system on edge before you play. Arrive at the course and the first tee in a relaxed state.

Warm up. Lightly stretch your muscles. Lay a club across the top of your back and slowly turn back and forth. Swing a couple of clubs. Then hit some shots to get a feel for your swing and making contact with the ball. If you have time, hit some short irons and middle irons, maybe a fairway wood and some drivers. Taper off with a few short pitch shots. Don't overdo and wear yourself out. And don't practice. Think play shots. That's what you're getting ready to do. Then go to the practice green and hit some chip shots and a few putts to get a feel for your stroke and the speed of the putting surface.

If your course doesn't have practice facilities, at least do your stretching. Then swing easily on the first few shots as you acquire some feel.

How to tee a ball

Your ball may be placed on a wooden peg called a tee at the start of each hole (although it's not mandatory). You must tee the *ball* between the front and outside of the markers and within two club-lengths behind them. Your feet may be outside this defined area.

The ball may be teed anywhere between the markers and to within two club lengths to the rear of the marker.

If you're using a driver, a good rule of thumb is to tee the ball so that the center of the ball is at the top of your club. With a fairway club, tee it slightly lower. That's so you can *sweep* the ball with those clubs. For an iron, when you'll be making a more downward swing, tee the ball at ground level so you give yourself a perfect lie.

How to mark your ball

On the green, you're allowed to mark your ball and clean it, and you have to mark it if it lies in the path of someone else's putt. Simply place a marker—a coin is the accepted thing—*behind* the ball and lift the ball. If your ball is in line with someone else's putt and you are asked to move your marker, be sure to mark the ball first, then move the coin one or more putterhead-lengths. This is not a big deal when playing with friends in a fun game, but it's the rule for tournament play. And don't forget to replace your marker in the right spot before you putt.

A coin placed behind the ball is the most common form of marking your spot on the green.

How to tend the flagstick

If you are asked to tend the flagstick while someone else is putting, here are a few simple rules:

❑ Avoid stepping in another player's line. Hold the flagstick at arm's length so you stand as far away from the hole as possible. If the wind is blowing, hold the flag so it doesn't flutter.

❏ Stand so your shadow doesn't fall across the line of the player's putt.

❏ Be sure the flagstick is loose so it doesn't stick when you try to pull it out. If a player's putt strikes the flagstick, it's a penalty.

❏ Remove the flagstick immediately after the putt has been struck.

❏ When you set the flagstick on the green, do it gently. Don't drop it. Somebody may have to putt over the indentation.

Watching where you step and stand is important when tending the flagstick.

How to dress

Sensibly. That's the answer. Golf courses are not very stuffy places, but good taste is always in vogue. Observe how others at your course normally dress. A golf shirt (with collar) and slacks for men are a good bet everywhere. Shorts of appropriate length are usually okay these days. A golf blouse and skirt, slacks or shorts are fine for women at most places. Make sure your clothing is reasonably loose-fitting so it doesn't bind you during the swing.

If invited to play at a private club, ask your host about the dress code.

Sure, you can wear a loin-cloth or a sarong if you want, but somebody might politely usher you off the premises. And hob-nailed boots or those funny sneaks with the big rubber ribs are out. The greenkeeper will have you out of there in a heartbeat.

If you are invited to play at a private club, ask your host about the dress code. Some still require skirts for women and ban shorts for men....okay, some of them *are* a little stuffy.

How to play in hot weather

Preparing for any kind of weather conditions is mostly a matter of common sense. When it's hot, and particularly if it's humid, wear light-colored cotton clothing that fits loosely, particularly your shirt. Wear a cap, hat or visor to keep the sun off your head and your eyes.

Stand or walk in the shade whenever possible.

Drink plenty of water before and throughout the round to prevent dehydration (this is good advice even if it's not particularly hot). Avoid drinks with sugar in them, and especially avoid alcohol. That cold beer will taste mighty good, but it will be mighty bad for your body, not to mention your game.

Avoid heavy meals before you play. Fruit or a light snack is best, and an apple or banana or raisins in your bag will help during the round.

Carry a towel to dry your hands. If you wear a glove, take along an extra one or two in case the first one soaks through. Douse your hands, head and neck with a cool, wet towel periodically.

How to play in cold weather

Dress in a few layers of lighter clothing—say, thermal underwear, a long-sleeved turtleneck and a sweater—rather than one heavy, bulky garment. That will keep you warm and still let you swing freely, and you can strip piece-by-piece if it gets warmer during the round. Keeping your hands warm is critical. Keep your hands in your pocket or in a pair of warm mittens whenever you can. A hand warmer, available in sporting goods departments, will do the best job of all.

Whenever possible, walk, don't ride. You avoid the wind-chill factor if you keep your blood moving.

How to play in rain

My wife once complained that she had to play in a club tournament in the rain and she didn't own a rainsuit. I promptly bought her one, and shortly thereafter we went on a golf vacation. As we were getting ready to leave the hotel room one morning, I looked at the threatening skies outside and told her to make sure she had her new rainsuit. She said, "I didn't bring it. There's a difference between having to play in the rain and choosing to play, and I don't *choose* to play in the rain."

Sound advice, perhaps, but if you have to or choose to play in wet weather, the first rule is to keep everything as dry as possible. Buy a good, lightweight rainsuit that breathes and is big enough to let you swing freely. Obviously stick an umbrella in your bag. Carry some towels and extra gloves in your bag. Towel off your club handles before every shot, and change gloves whenever one gets wet.

When everything gets so slippery that you can't make a decent swing, maybe the bar and grill is the best alternative. Again, if there is lightning around, that's the first alternative....and take it quickly!

How to care for your tools

Golf equipment costs money, so take care of it and make it last as long as possible. There's really not a lot to it.

If you had to or chose to play in the rain and your shoes got wet, stuff them with wadded-up newspapers and let them dry naturally. Don't put them in front of a radiator or the fireplace. When they're dry, give them a good polishing.

Keep your clubs dry and clean. Never put them away either wet or dirty. You know that water causes rust, even on treated metal heads. So does the acid in dirt. Use a reasonably stiff brush (but not one that will scratch) and water to wash the clubheads, and don't overlook the grooves in the face. Wipe off your grips with a damp towel, and you can even bathe and brush them periodically, making sure to wipe them dry. When they get worn and smooth, have them replaced by your pro or a club-repair shop.

If you wear a glove, smooth it out and put it back in the envelope it came in after each round. It will last a lot longer. Carry two or three and alternate them.

Keep your golf balls clean during a round. Not only will they putt and fly truer, they'll stay shiny and white longer.

Investing a little time in maintenance will save you a lot in replacement costs.

How to pack for a golf trip

Pack the way you usually do for any vacation, but in selecting your clothing take into account that you'll be spending time on the golf course as well as dining and dancing. Prepare for surprises in the weather. No matter where your destination, a sweater, some heavier slacks, a rainsuit and maybe a windbreaker is always a good idea.

You don't need a bag as big as the pros carry, but it should be sturdy enough to withstand the airport baggage handlers. Make sure it has a hood, and buy a bag cover for protection. Carry enough balls and gloves to last, because they may cost more where you're going, especially if it's a resort. And take along an extra pair of shoes if you can in case of rain.

A golf scorecard is really a simple thing to keep; a lot easier than in bowling. The card usually contains the yardage and par for each particular hole, plus the total yardage and par for each nine and the 18. This information is given for each set of tees on the course.

As you'll note, the different tees are normally designated by color, e.g. blue, white, gold, etc. The handicap number of each hole is listed to let you know where you give or get strokes.

If you are playing a match, these numbers also indicate the relative difficulty of the holes. Note that the handicap numbers are different for most forward tees which are

Par		4	3	4	4	3	4	5	5	4	
Blue		435	208	370	450	165	386	608	456	382	3
White		415	200	363	430	160	381	563	448	320	32
Gold		415	200	280	430	160	305	490	357	320	29
Handicap		5	15	11	3	17	7	1	9	13	
DAN	Hcp 16	5	4	4	5	3	5	5	6	4	4
JESSICA	21	6	4	5	5	3	6	6	5	5	4
Hole		1	2	3	4	5	6	7	8	9	0
MARY	15	5	3	4	6	4	4	5	4	5	4
ROY	18	5	5	6	6	4	6	6	5	6	4
Handicap		5	15	13	11	17	7	1	3	9	
Red		397	159	280	406	131	305	490	357	299	28
Par		5	3	4	5	3	4	5	5	4	

scorecard

normally shown at the bottom of the card and generally termed the red tees.

There is a space for the name of each player in the group and usually a place to note his or her handicap. And there are boxes to write in the scores for each player on each hole, and for the nine- and 18-hole totals. Usually there is a box after the 18-hole total to enter a player's handicap and another to record the net score for the round.

Most scorecards also have a place for the person keeping the scorecard to sign his or her name. There's also a space for another player to "attest" to the accuracy of the scores. This is important for future handicapping purposes.

	5	4	4	4	3	4	4	4	35	71		
0	534	390	385	420	135	332	415	406	3157	6617		
5	522	385	373	410	130	320	397	400	3072	6352		
5	455	385	312	410	130	320	351	400	2898	5855		
3	2	12	4	6	16	14	10	8				
	7	5	4	4	3	5	4	5	40	81	10	71
	5	6	6	5	5	4	5	5	45	90	21	69

	11	12	13	14	15	16	17	18	In	Tot	Hcp	Net
	6	5	5	4	4	4	5	5	42	82	15	67
	7	6	4	5	3	6	4	5	43	92	18	74
2	14	4	12	16	8	6	10					
9	455	327	312	399	117	288	351	344	2712	5536		
	5	4	4	5	3	4	4	4	36	74		

Attest *Roy Smith*

Date: 9/12/92

Scorer: *Dan Jones*

How to watch a golf tournament

Attending a professional golf tournament or a good amateur event can be both fun and instructive. It shows you how well the game can be played and probably will inspire you to play it better. It can even help you do that if you pay attention.

First, let common sense rule. Dress appropriately. Wear sensible, rubber-soled walking shoes. Don't wear your golf spikes and for Heaven's sake don't wear spike heels. Wear clothing appropriate for the weather....and expect it to change. Especially be prepared for rain.

Know the rules for spectators. Cameras are not allowed at professional events once the competition starts, and usually no coolers are permitted. You're expected to be courteous, keeping quiet while golfers are playing shots nearby, just as in your own Saturday group. Booing and heckling is considered bad form.

And don't drink to excess. It can be embarrassing, costly and painful—alcohol works quickly in the hot sun.

There are several ways to watch. You can follow your favorite player or players hole-by-hole. You can find one spot and stay there all day to see all the players come through—dramatic holes or the 18th green are the best. Or find a place where you can see several holes—the tees, fairways or greens—with very little walking.

Finally, and most important if you want to improve your own game, watch carefully how the top players perform. Go to the practice area and watch how they swing. If possible, pick out a player of your own size and body type and see how he or she does it. Pay close attention to the rhythm, pace and overall activity of their swings. Especially note their strategy on the course. That's where most scores are made or ruined.   ∎

Other Publications

If you would like to know more about what's covered in this chapter, here is some additional suggested reading.

Golf Fore Beginners: The Fundamentals (Stephen Ruthenberg, Published 1992 by RGS Pub)

Golf Schools: The Complete Guide (Barbara Wolf, Paperback, Published 1997 by golf.com Press)

GAMES GOLFERS PLAY

G olf is a compelling game by itself. It's fun just to go out alone and knock the ball around. It's even more fun to play games within the game, by yourself or with others. Most of us like to compete, and no sport better lends itself to a variety of competition than golf. That enhances the enjoyment for beginner and expert alike. Besides that, you can whip your friends out of a few bucks if you have a good day.

Let's look at how golfers play games.

Match vs. Stroke Play

There are two basic forms of competition, *match play* and *stroke play* (sometimes referred to as *medal play*). In match play, the competition is on a hole-by-hole basis. Whichever individual or team wins the most holes during the round is the winner. The overall score of either doesn't matter. In stroke play, overall score at the end of the round or the tournament—which can be two, three or four rounds and sometimes even longer—determines the winner.

You can play either way by yourself. You won't win or lose any money, but you can get a lot of satisfaction and learn how to play better. Set a stroke goal for nine holes or 18 holes (or four holes, for that matter) and see if you can beat it. Or play a match against par or bogey or double-bogey, depending on your skill level. If you're playing a match against bogey and make a bogey on a hole, you tie. If you make par, you win. If you make double bogey or worse, you lose. It's the same as if you had a real opponent.

Better Ball

The most common form of informal play in the United States is four-ball, often known as better-ball. It's a match-play format in which two players compete against two other players. The better score of the two players on a team counts on each hole against the better score of the other two players. If you and your partner each make five on a hole and one of the other team makes a six but the other one makes a four, that teams wins the hole.

The game is almost always played on a net basis, using handicaps. If you don't have handicaps and you're playing with friends who know each other's games, you can divide up the teams pretty evenly or arbitrarily decide how many handicap strokes will be given each player.

Variations include "low ball-low total," in which a point is awarded to a team for the low score on a hole and another point is given to a team if its total score of two balls is lower than the other; or "low ball-high ball," in which a point is won by the team with the lowest individual score and a point is lost by the team with the highest individual score.

The Nassau

The usual game is a Nassau. Let's say it's a $2 Nassau. The team that wins the most holes or the most points on the front nine wins $2 a person. The team that wins on the back nine gets $2 each. The team with the most overall holes or points wins another $2 each. You could win or lose $6 on the round.

The Press

But there's more. There's a devilish little device called the press. A press is simply a new bet. Usually it's called by a team whenever it is two holes down, although you can set rules that allow the losing team to press at any time before a new hole starts. It means a new bet is started while the old bet continues. If your team is two holes down and you press, then win the next hole, you and your partner are now one down on the original bet and one up on the press. If you win another hole before your opponents do, the first bet is even and you're two up on the press. At that point, your opponents can press if they choose, which means you now have three bets going. You can refuse the press, but it's not considered good form.

The presses continue for nine holes, at the end of which everything starts over. If you've lost the front nine, you can press the back nine, which means you're now playing it for $4. If a team gets two down on the back nine, it can issue a single press or a double press, which means the new bet is either for $2 or $4. If it gets to the point where a team has lost the overall bet—for example, it is three holes down overall with two holes to play—it can press the 18, adding still another bet.

You know, you can get in a lot of trouble that way if you're stubborn and playing badly.

Six-Six-Six

A variation of four-ball is six-six-six, the players switching partners every six holes and adding up the bets at the end. Another version of that is to play six holes as a four-ball, each player playing his own ball, six holes as foursomes and six holes as a scramble (the latter two will be explained shortly).

Garbage

Within the basic game, many players will add on bets called "garbage" or "trash." For instance, gross *birdies* can be worth $1 (or whatever amount you choose). *Greenies* or *proxes*, which go to the player who gets closest to the hole in the regulation number of strokes on par-3 holes, can be worth 50 cents. Greenies also can be played on par-5 holes. Almost always they are played as "carryovers," which means that if there is no greenie on the first par-3 or par-5, the next one is worth double, and so on. You can play greenies on every hole if you like. That version is usually played as "progressive" greenies, with the point going to the player who gets closest to the hole in the fewest strokes, even if it's not in regulation.

There is more garbage. You can play *sandies*, which means your team wins 50 cents whenever one of you makes par from out of the sand (or bogey, or whatever standard you set). You can play *barkies*, one of which is earned whenever you hit a tree and still make par. There are *Hogans* for hitting the fairway, hitting the green and making par or better (named after the great Ben Hogan, who did that most of the time). Or *Arnies*, which are earned after you've missed the fairway, missed the green and still made par or better (named after the great Arnold Palmer, who did that a lot). There are *Watsons*, also known as *Crenshaws*, for chipping off the green for par or better, named for Tom Watson and Ben Crenshaw, who are masters at that sort of thing. You can win a *gurglie* for hitting the ball in the water and still making par.

Bingo Bango Bungo

A popular game in many areas is *bingo, bango, bungo* (or *bingle, bangle, bungle*), in which a point each is awarded for first on the green, closest to the hole and first into the hole. That can be played as garbage or as the game itself.

Las Vegas

If you want to get into higher math, play Las Vegas. In this one, each score on a side determines a team's score for the hole. If you make a 4 and your partner makes 6, your team's score is 46. If your two opponents each make 5, their total is 55 and you win nine points. The low score always comes first, except when one team makes a birdie. Then the other team's high score comes first. It could turn a 48 into an 84! Be careful how much you make each point worth because they can add up quickly.

There are others, but you get the idea. If you get carried away, the garbage can be worth more than the basic bet itself. But that's the fun of it. Most of us can't threaten the course record every time out. There might be a bad hole or two (or three or four) that will ruin the total score. But in match play and with the side games, we start over again on every hole and every shot and we have fun to the very end.

Three Player Games

There are many games for three players. *Syndicates* or *skins* or *scats* may be the most common. A player who has the low score on a hole wins a designated amount. If two tie, all tie. You can play carryovers or not, as you choose.

Another fun game is *Hawk*. The players alternate honors every three holes. The player designated No. 1 tees off on the first hole, No. 2 on the second, No. 3 on the third and thereafter in the same order. The Hawk, the player with the honor, is allowed to choose another player as his partner after everybody hits his drive. Obviously he will choose the player in the best position, or perhaps the one with a handicap stroke on the hole. Or he may choose to play the other two alone. If he wins, he gets two points. If he loses, he loses a point to each of the others. Add them up at the end.

Either of these games and others obviously can be played by four golfers.

The list of games for two, three and four or more players goes on forever. The book referenced at the end of this chapter contains many of them. But don't worry. One of your playing companions will always bring up a new game and a new way to have fun.

A word here—the U.S. Golf Association has no problem with gambling as long as it's just between you and your friends. Nobody really cares whether they condone it or not. It's going to happen if you want it to, and that's okay if it adds to your fun. But betting on golf is just like any other betting. Don't bet more than you can afford to lose....but you already knew that.

The Scramble

There are many other forms of competition. One variation becoming more popular in the U.S. is the scramble. The basic form of scramble is to have everyone drive, select the best one and have everyone hit the second shot from there and so on into the hole. It can be played with two-person teams or by teams of four or more playing against each other at match. Or it can be played as stroke competition. It's especially fun to play when you are learning. You get a chance to hit good shots and usually don't have to play your bad ones.

Foursomes

Foursomes is a form of play more popular in Great Britain and Ireland and other parts of the world than in the United States, but it is sometimes played here. In its purest form it is two-person teams playing one ball, alternating shots. One partner tees off on the even tees, the other partner on the odd tees and then they alternate shots until the ball is holed.

A variation is called Chapman or Pinehurst. Both players drive, each hits the other's ball on the second shot and then one ball is chosen to be played into the hole with alternate strokes.

How about tournaments? You may not be ready for the U.S. Open or the state amateur championship yet. But most courses and cities have tournaments broken into flights, which divide players by skill level. You may or may not have to have a handicap index. Check with your professional.

League play is a popular form of tournament competition. Companies sponsor them, courses sponsor them, cities and towns sponsor them. Again, ask around and find out how you can get on a team when you feel comfortable enough with your game.

Jump right in. You may be nervous, but don't worry about it. In the long run, competition will make you a better player. And, for now or forever, just remember that you're doing the same thing everybody else is doing—having fun playing games within the game.   ■

Other Publications

If you would like to know more about what's covered in this chapter, here is some additional suggested reading.

GOLFGAMES: The Side Games We Play and Wager (Rich Ussak, Paperback, Published 1993 by Contemporary Books)

Golf Games Within the Game: 200 Fun Ways Players Can Add Variety and Challenge to Their Game (Linda Valentine and Margie Hubbard, Paperback, Published 1992 by Perigee)

THE LANGUAGE OF GOLF

L
ike most sports, golf has its own terminology. If you're new in the game, the language can be as foreign as Sanskrit.

Because golf is so old and has spread throughout the world, the terms are rich, varied and colorful. The origins of many are obscured by time. There are conflicting stories on the beginnings of others.

You learned many terms in earlier chapters. What follows is a list of other common ones and some of the more colorful expressions. There are many that aren't listed, and the language of golf is constantly changing. You'll pick it up as you play more, but this will give you a head start.

Scoring Terms

Par—The number of strokes an expert golfer would be expected to take on a given hole or for the round. You don't want to be feeling under par, but on a golf course "under par" is good. It probably comes from the Latin *par*, meaning equal.

Bogey—One stroke over par on any hole. Bogey actually was the original par, the score to be sought. It may have been established in 1890 by Hugh Rotherham, an Englishman who got tired of adding up every stroke in his round and decided on an imaginary golfer who was a "uniformly steady golfer but never over-brilliant" as a standard or ground score to play against on each hole. Some months later, a Major Charles Wellman, while playing against Rotherham's club,

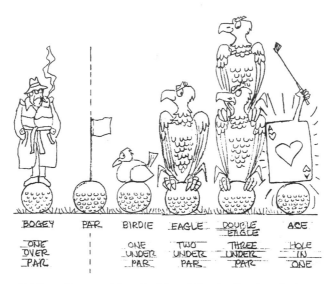

BOGEY	PAR	BIRDIE	EAGLE	DOUBLE EAGLE	ACE
ONE OVER PAR		ONE UNDER PAR	TWO UNDER PAR	THREE UNDER PAR	HOLE IN ONE

Golf has its own rich, colorful and fascinating terminology.

exclaimed, "This player of yours is a regular bogey man." And so it became. The major may have been promoted at some point, because a Colonel Bogey looms large in the legend of the term. As players got better over the years and more began to beat bogey regularly, the word *par* began to be used as the new standard and *bogey* came to represent one over par.

Double-bogey—Two over par on a hole.

Triple-bogey—Three over on a hole.

Birdie—One stroke under par on a hole. The origin is unclear. *Bird* was once used in 13th-century England to describe an exceptionally smart or accomplished person. It may have first been used in connection with golf at the Atlantic City Country Club in New Jersey in 1903 when an Abe Smith hit his second shot close to the hole on a par-4 and exclaimed, "That was one bird of a shot!"

Eagle—Two under par on a hole. It's rarer and more exotic than a birdie, so the extension is obvious.

Double-eagle—Three under par on a hole. Also known as an *albatross*, which is even more rare and more beautiful than an eagle.

Ace—Also known as a hole-in-one, it means you've holed out in one stroke. It almost always happens on a par-3 hole (which also makes it an eagle) but has been known to occur on par-4 holes (in which case it's a double-eagle).

Dormie—If you are as many holes "up" or ahead in a match as there are holes left to play, you are dormie (your opponent is not dormie, although the expression is commonly misused that way). It comes from the French *endormi,* meaning asleep, or the Latin *dormio,* to sleep. The implication is that you can relax because you can't lose the match even if you fall asleep. That's not really the case, however. You could lose in overtime.

Terms About Shots

Mulligan—A second ball allowed, without penalty, to a player who has driven badly off the first tee (also sometimes known as a *lunch ball).* The term is popularly ascribed to a Canadian, David Mulligan, who was allowed an extra shot in return for driving his friends to their weekly game at the St. Lambert Club near Montreal. Another version has it that Mulligan would invariably mis-hit his first drive and beg his partners for another. Reportedly, Mulligan later moved to New York and joined Winged Foot, where to this day a Mulligan is common practice. There are other versions of its origin. The rule-making bodies recognize none of them nor the Mulligan itself.

Chip—Also *chip shot,* one that is struck from near the green with a medium-lofted club. It's low, doesn't travel very high or very far in the air and rolls a long way after landing on the green.

Pitch—Also *pitch shot,* one struck from around the green or less than full-shot distance that goes high and doesn't roll all that far after landing.

Bump and run—A low shot played from off the green that lands short of the putting surface and bounces and rolls, hopefully close to the hole. It's most effective when the ground is firm.

Putt—A shot made with a putter on (or off) the putting surface that rolls along the ground.

Fade—A shot that curves slightly to the right.

Slice—A shot that curves a great deal to the right.

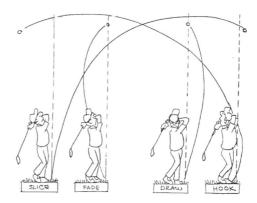

When talking golf, it's well to know the difference between a slice and a fade ... or a hook and a draw.

Draw—A shot that curves slightly left.

Hook—A shot that curves a lot to the left.

Top—To hit a shot above the center of the ball. It bounces along the ground and is not to be desired. Also known as a *skull.*

Duck hook—A shot hit to the left and low that curves sharply farther left. It's much worse than a hook. Also known as a *snap hook* or *snap.*

Thin shot—A shot hit just slightly better than a top. It gets in the air but doesn't travel very high or very far, except when you do it around the green. Then it goes too far. Also known as a *bladed* or *bellied shot.*

Fat shot—A shot in which the club strikes the ground before the ball. It doesn't go far enough. Also known as a *chili-dip.* Also *obese.* If it's a very fat shot, you *laid the sod over it* or *stuck it in the ground.*

Stub—A short shot, usually a chip, that you hit fat or stick the club in the ground.

Skied shot—One hit too high and weakly. Sometimes known as a *pop-up,* or *rainmaker.*

Toed shot—The ball was hit with the toe end of the club.

Heeled shot—The ball was hit with the heel portion of the club. Sometimes called an *Oral Roberts* (see if you can figure that out).

Shank—A definite no-no, it's a shot struck with the hosel of an iron club that squirts wildly to the right. Some golfers don't even like to hear the word used. Also known as a *lateral pitchout* or a *heavy slice.*

Whiff—It's when you miss the ball altogether. Other terms include *silent shot* or *no noise on the ball.*

Worm-burner—A shot that skims the ground for awhile and then rolls. Also known as a *blue darter.*

Wind-cheater—A shot that is hit solidly and low into the wind.

OB or Oscar Bravo—A shot hit out of bounds. Also *Oscar Brown,* whoever either one of them is.

Lipout—A putt that travels part way around the lip or edge of the hole and stays out. Also can be used as a verb, as in *lipped it out.*

Slam dunk—A putt that goes into the hole while traveling at a great rate of speed, hitting the back of the cup and plopping in.

Snake—A very long putt that goes in. Also known as a *field goal.*

Other Common Expressions

Blocks—The tee markers. Also *tee blocks.*

Putting clock—Another term for the practice putting green.

On the dance floor—The putting surface, as when your ball is on it.

Get up and down—to make a shot from off the green and sink the putt.

Scramble—In this case, not the form of competition but to recover from missing the green, as in getting it up and down.

Carry—The distance your ball travels in the air before landing, as in "How long is the carry over that pond?"

Gimmie—A shot or putt that ends up so close to the hole that your opponent concedes the next stroke. Also known as a *kick-in.*

In the leather—A shot or putt that ends up close to the hole. Originally this was meant to be within the length of the handle on your putter. Now it's interpreted as being within the length of your putterhead to the bottom of the handle. At any rate, your opponent probably will concede.

Stiff—When your shot to the green ends up close to the hole, within gimmie or kick-in range, you've hit it stiff.

Fried egg—A ball that is semi-buried in a sand bunker with the sand spread out in a ridge around it.

Plugged lie—A ball that is deeply imbedded in the sand.

Hit a house—What you say when you hit a chip shot or putt too hard and it's going way past the hole. It won't do any good, though.

Hit it sideways—What you say when you didn't play well.

Whipped it around—What you say when you did play well, and may you get a chance to say it often.   ■

Other Publications

If you would like to know more about what's covered in this chapter, here is some additional suggested reading.

Historical Dictionary of Golfing Terms: From 1500 to the Present (Peter Davies, Published 1992 by Michael Kesend Pub Ltd.)

14
THE JOY IS IN
THE EXPERIENCE

Some time ago, John Merchant was sitting in the grill room at a golf course with a beer and his playing companions of the day. John is black, which he has always been. He is an attorney, which he has not always been. He is a member of a private club, which he has not always been. He grew up playing public courses. He carries a single-digit handicap, but like all of us he was not that good in the beginning. He was at the time one of the newest members of the United States Golf Association's Executive Committee, the group that runs the organization. All of which is not really important, except that it shows John has been through everything as a golfer.

He was swapping stories about the round, the good shots and bad, the putts that had gone in and those that had not. He had not played up to expectations that day, but at one point he leaned back, smiled and said, "This is what it's all about, isn't it? This is the fun of it all."

It is. We're always happy with our successes. We seldom talk about our failures and disappointments. When is the last time you heard somebody exult-

Much like life, golf is largely a matter of recalling your successes.

ing over losing his job or his latest root canal?

But in golf there are no successes or failures. Certainly you win and you lose, you do better or worse than you wanted. But the joy of golf is in the experience, in the playing of the game. Good shots and bad are of no account at the end of the day, sitting over a drink with friends. The only thing that counts is the joy you had in playing all of them....and remembering them.

This is the joy that you and all of us have in store as we continue to play the greatest game in the world. Experiencing, recalling, laughing about it with our friends and experiencing again.

That's the fun of it all.

■

INDEX

A

Addressing the ball   24
Aiming the club   24

B

Ball marks
    repairing   55
Ball position   25
Bunkers   35

C

Course Type
    executive   16
    par-3   15
    regulation   16

E

Equipment
    golf balls   48
    grip size   47
    irons   46
    lie   47
    loft   46
    shaft flex   47
    woods   46

F

Fairway   34
Flagstick   37
Fringe   38

G

Games
    better ball   80
    bingo bango bungo   82
    foursomes   83
    garbage   81
    las vegas   82
    match play   79
    nassau   80
    press   80
    scramble   83
    six-six-six   81
    stroke play   79
    three player   82
Golf courses
    private   39
    public   39
    resort   39
Golf personnel   42
Golf vacations   42
Green   38
Gripping the club   22

H _____

Handicap
    how to get one   66

L _____

Language   86
Learn to play   31
Learning sources   30
Learning to play
    caring for your equipment   75
    how to dress   73
    how to tend flagstick   72
    marking ball   72
    teeing the ball   72

O _____

Out of bounds   35

P _____

Posture   25
Practice
    how to   28
Practice area   38

R _____

Range
    driving   14
    golf   14
    practice   14
Rough   35
Rules
    balls   45
    casual water   62
    clubs   45
    equipment   45
    hazards
        bunker   60
        water   59
    honor   59
    how to drop   62
    lost ball   61
    obstructions   61
    out of bounds   60
    playing courteously   54
        bunkers   55
        playing through   54
        replacing divots   54
    playing safely   52
    provisional ball   61
    the game   58
    the stroke   58
    unplayable lie   61

S _____

Slope System   69
Stance   25
Swinging the club   26

T _____

Teacher
    How to get the most
    out of   29
Tee time
    how to get one   40
Teeing ground   34

W _____

Water hazards   36
    lateral   36

Y _____

Yardage marker   36

APPENDIX

GOLF SCHOOLS

I n addition to local golf professionals, there are scores of golf schools across the country that are excellent sources of instruction and education.

Following is a listing of golf schools and camps courtesy of ShawGuides. This listing is continually updated on their web site: http://www.shawguides.com/golf.

Please note that the fact that a golf school appears on the following list does not imply that it has been certified or is being otherwise recommended by the NGF. It is important, therefore, that you thoroughly check out a school's references and other credentials before making a commitment. All of the schools on this list should be more than happy to help you in this matter.

Alabama

Alabama Crimson Tide Golf Academy
1655 McFarland Blvd. N., Ste. 116
Tuscaloosa, AL 35406
Phone: 205-348-0383
Fax: 205-752-0675

Arizona

Arizona State Golf Academy
Arizona State University, 306 ICA Bldg.
Tempe, AZ 85287-2505
Phone: 602-965-2603
Fax: 602-965-9480

Bobby Eldridge Golf School
PO Box 26073
Phoenix, AZ 85068
Phone: 800-353-7434
Fax: 602-942-0122

Contact Golf School
4435 E. Paradise Village Pkwy, So.
Phoenix, AZ 85032
Phone: 602-953-0604
Fax: 602-953-3297
E-mail: mtrimbe@ash.campus.mci.net

Golf Schools of Scottsdale
La Posada Resort
4949 E. Lincoln Dr., Ste. 102
Scottsdale, AZ 85253
Phone: 800-356-6678

**Jim McLean Golf Academy
at Legend Trail Golf Club**
9462 Legendary Ln
Scottsdale, AZ 85262
Phone: 602-488-2498
Fax: 602-488-6968
E-mail: doral.scott

John Jacobs' Golf Schools
7825 East Redfield Rd.
Scottsdale, AZ 85260-6977
Phone: 800-472-5007/602-991-8587
Fax: 602-991-8243

**Mundus Institute School of Golf
Course Management**
4745 N. 7th St.
Phoenix, AZ 85014
Phone: 800-835-3727/602-248-8548
Fax: 602-234-1910

Sonoran Desert Golf School
3252 E. McKellips Rd.
Mesa, AZ 85213
Phone: 602-924-1350
Fax: 602-924-7877

Stratton/Scottsdale Golf School
Box 6349
Scottsdale, AZ 85261
Phone: 800-238-2424/602-998-4039

Swing Masters Golf Schools
5110 N. 44 St. L-215
Phoenix, AZ 85018
Phone: 800-752-9162/602-952-8484
Fax: 612-952-9122

Arkansas

Jack Fleck College of Golf Knowledge
Lil' Bit A Heaven Golf Club
Rte.1, Box 140
Magazine, AR 72943
Phone: 501-969-2203
Fax: 501-969-2797

California

Aviara Golf Academy by Kip Puterbaugh
7447 Batiquitos Dr.
Carlsbad, CA 92009
Phone: 800-433-7468/619-438-4539
Fax: 619-438-7391

Bruce Baird's Monterey Golf School
43926 Rembrandt St.
Lancaster, CA 93535
Phone: 800-894-9593
Fax: 805-948-3486
E-mail: baird@weteachgolf.com
URL: http://www.weteachgolf.com

Carmel Valley Ranch Golf School
One Old Ranch Rd.
Carmel, CA 93923
Phone: 408-626-2510
Fax: 408-626-2532

Dean Reinmuth School of Golf
Carlton Oaks Country Club, 9200 Inwood Dr.
Santee, CA 92071
Phone: 619-562-9755
Fax: 619-562-6864

Diamond Golf Schools
100 S. Sunrise Way, #418
Palm Springs, CA 92262
Phone: 800-847-4539
Fax: 619-416-1412
E-mail: diamondgolf.earthlink.net

Glenn Monday School of Golf
460 W. Holly St.
El Segundo, CA 90245
Phone: 310-322-8924
Fax: 310-322-8924

Golf University at San Diego
Rancho Bernardo Inn
17550 Bernardo Oaks Dr.
San Diego, CA 92128
Phone: 800-426-0966/619-485-8880
Fax: 619-485-9423

Haggin Oaks Junior Golf Camps
Haggin Oaks Golf Course, 3645 Fulton Ave.
Sacramento, CA 95821
Phone: 916-481-4653
Fax: 916-481-3440

La Costa Golf School
La Costa Hotel and Spa
2100 Costa del Mar Rd.
Carlsbad, CA 92009
Phone: 800-653-7888/619-438-9111
Fax: 619-438-3758

NIKE Jr. Golf Camps
919 Sir Francis Drake Blvd.
Kentfield, CA 94904
Phone: 800-645-3226/415-459-0459
Fax: 415-459-1453
URL: http://www.us-sportscamps.com

Northstar-at-Tahoe Golf School
PO Box 129
Truckee, CA 96160
Phone: 800-466-6784/916-562-1010
Fax: 916-562-2215
E-mail: nstar@sierra.net

Ojai Golf Academy
Ojai Valley Inn & Country Club, Country
   Club Rd.
Ojai, CA 93023
Phone: 805-646-5511/800-422-6524

Professional Golfers Career College
P.O. Box 682
Murrieta, CA 92564
Phone: 800-877-4380/909-698-4380
Fax: 909-698-4384

Sonoma Golf School
Sonoma, CA Phone: 707-939-0523
E-mail: krismoe@wco.com
URL: http://www.sonomagolfschool.com

THE School of Golf
Singing Hills Country Club & Resort
3007 Dehasa Road
El Cajon, CA 92019
Phone: 800-457-5568/619-442-3425
Fax: 619-442-9574

Colorado

Craft-Zavichas Golf School
600 Dittmer Ave.
Pueblo, CO 81005
Phone: 800-858-9633/719-564-2616

Falcon Golf Camp
c/o Dept. of Athletics, United States Air
   Force Academy
Colorado Springs, CO 80840
Phone: 719-472-2280/800-666-8723
Fax: 719-472-2599

Rocky Mountain Family Golf School
Box 456
Gunnison, CO 81230
Phone: 303-641-0451/800-758-RMGS

Sheraton Steamboat Resort Golf School
Sheraton Steamboat Resort & Conference
   Center, P.O
Steamboat Springs, CO 80477
Phone: 303-879-2220, #1071
Fax: 303-879-7686

Vail Golf School
1778 Vail Valley Drive
Vail, CO 81657
Phone: 970-479-2260
Fax: 970-479-2355

Connecticut

Golf Digest Schools
5520 Park Ave.
Trumbull, CT 06611-0395
Phone: 800-243-6121/203-373-7128
Fax: 203-373-7088
E-mail: GolfDigestSchools@msn.com
URL: http://www.golf.com/golfdigest/schools

Offense-Defense Golf Camp
P.O. Box 6
Easton, CT 06612
Phone: 800-T2-GREEN/203-256-9844
Fax: 203-255-5666
URL: http://www.offensedefensegolf.com

Florida

Academy of Golf at PGA National
PGA Natl Resort & Spa
1000 Ave. of the Champions
Palm Beach Gardens, FL 33418
Fax: 407-624-8904

Amelia Island Plantation Golf School
Amelia Island Plantation
P.O. Box 3000
Amelia Island, FL 32034
Phone: 800-874-6878/904-277-5976
Fax: 904-277-5189

America's Favorite Golf Schools
P.O. Box 3325
Ft. Pierce, FL 34948
Phone: 800-365-6640/407-461-9818
Fax: 407-461-5636

Arnold Palmer Golf Academy
9000 Bay Hill Blvd.
Orlando, FL 32819-4899
Phone: 800-523-5999/407-876-8008
Fax: 407-856-3671

Back in the Swing Golf School
910 SE 4th Ave.
Pompano Beach, FL 33060
Phone: 954-733-2112
Fax: 954-786-0156

Cape Coral Golf & Tennis Resort
  Golf School
Cape Coral Golf & Tennis Resort
4003 Palm Tree Blvd.
Cape Coral, FL 33904
Phone: 941-542-7879, #3191
Fax: 941-542-4694

David Leadbetter Golf Academy
5500 34th St. West
Bradenton, FL 34210
Phone: 800-424-DLGA

Deer Creek Golf School
2801 Country Club Blvd.
Deerfield Beach, FL 33442
Phone: 954-429-3569/954-429-0623

Dennis Meyer's Golf School
PO Box 94
Estero, FL 33928-0094
Phone: 800-445-4554
Fax: 941-267-0302

Doral Golf Learning Center
  with Jim McLean
4400 NW 87th Ave.
Miami, FL 33178-2192
Phone: 800-72-DORAL/305-591-6409
Fax: 305-599-2890

Fellowship of Christian Athletes
  Junior Golf Camps
FCA Golf Ministry, P.O. Box 664
Ponte Vedra Beach, FL 32004
Phone: 904-273-9541
Fax: 904-285-1260

Gator Golf Camp
P.O. Box 14485
Gainesville, FL 32604-2485
Phone: 352-375-4683, #4720
Fax: 352-395-6228
E-mail: sarahj@gators.uaa.ufl.edu

Golf Academy of the South
307 Daneswood Way
Casselberry, FL 32707
Phone: 800-786-0108/407-699-1990
Fax: 407-699-6653

Golf Institute
Innisbrook Hilton Resort, P.O. Drawer
  1088
Tarpon Springs, FL 34286
Phone: 813-942-2000/5221
Fax: 813-942-5577

Grand Cypress Academy of Golf
Grand Cypress Resort
One N. Jacaranda Blvd.
Orlando, FL 32836
Phone: 800-835-7377/407-239-1975
Fax: 407-239-1998

Greg Ortman Golf Academy
P.O. Box 7010
Grenelefe, FL 33844
Phone: 941-421-0470
Fax: 941-421-0470

Ken Venturi Golf Academy
  at Grenelefe
State Rd. 546, Box 7010
Haines City, FL 33844
Phone: 800-543-7084/941-422-7511
Fax: 941-421-0470
URL: http://www.kenventuri.com

Nicklaus/Flick Golf School
11780 U.S. Hwy. #1
N. Palm Beach, FL 32082
Phone: 800-642-5528
Fax: 561-626-4104
URL: http://www.nicklaus.com

Paradise Golf Schools
936 N. Collier Blvd
Marco Island, FL 34145
Phone: 800-624-3543/941-394-5830
Fax: 941-394-7556
E-mail: pgsutd@aol.com
URL: http://www.golf-florida.com

Professional Golf Schools of America
4105 Luff St.
Panama City Beach, FL 32408
Phone: 800-447-2744
Fax: 407-743-6810

Ron Philo's School of Golf
3000 First Coast Hwy
Amelia Island, FL 32034
Phone: 904-277-5976
Fax: 904-277-5189

Saddlebrook Academy
5700 Saddlebrook Way
Wesley Chapel, FL 33543-4499
Phone: 813-973-1111
Fax: 813-991-4713

School of Relaxed Golf
University Park Country Club
7671 Park Blvd.
University Park, FL 34201
Phone: 813-359-9999
Fax: 813-351-7778

**Tee to Green Golf School
 & Jr. Golf Camp**
3103 Fla Coach Dr
Kissimmee, FL 34741
Phone: 407-847-2816
Fax: 407-847-6358

Toski-Battersby Golf Learning Center
1000 Coconut Creek Blvd.
Coconut Creek, FL 33066
Phone: 305-975-2045
Fax: 305-973-2389
E-mail: GBattAli@aol.com

Tour School
PO Box 3742
Winter Springs, FL 32708
Phone: 407-699-9486
E-mail: jciron@aol.com

United States Senior Golf Academy
P.O. Box 410339
Melbourne, FL 32941-0339
Phone: 800-654-5752
Fax: 407-729-9579

V.I.P. Golf Academy
2912 Par Rd.
Sebring, FL 33872
Phone: 800-673-7686
Fax: 941-655-0100

Georgia

Georgia Junior Golf Foundation, Inc.
121 Village Pkwy., Bldg. 3
Marietta, GA 30067-4061
Phone: 770-955-4272
Fax: 770-955-1156

Georgia School of Golf
7333 Lynch Rd.
Midland, GA 31820
Phone: 706-562-8111
Fax: 706-501-2065

Georgia Tech Golf Camp
150 Bobby Dodd Way, NW
Atlanta, GA 30332-0455
Phone: 404-894-0961
Fax: 404-894-1248
E-mail: abridges@at.gtaa.gatech.edu

Sorrell Golf School
1940 Flippen Rd.
Stockbridge, GA 30281
Phone: 770-957-8786/9554

Hawaii

Del Mar Golf College
2290 Kaanapali Parkway
Lahaina, HI 96761
Phone: 808-661-0488
Fax: 808-662-3121

Kapalua Golf Club
300 Kapalua Dr.
Kapalua, Maui, III 96761
Phone: 808-669-8820
Fax: 808-669-4956

Illinois

Eagle Ridge Golf Academy
Eagle Ridge Inn & Resort, P.O. Box 777
Galena, IL 61036
Phone: 800-892-2269/815-777-2444
Fax: 815-777-0445

**Illinois State University Redbird
 Golf Camp**
7130 Horton Field House
Normal, IL 61761
Phone: 309-438-3635
Fax: 309-438-2323

Natural Golf Schools
2400 W. Hassell Rd., Ste. 370
Hoffman Estates, IL 60195
Phone: 888-NAT-GOLF
E-mail: oneaxis@ix.netcom.com
URL: http://www.naturalgolfer.com

University of Illinois Summer Camps
1817 S. Neil St., #201
Champaign, IL 61820
Phone: 217-244-7278
Fax: 217-244-0035
E-mail: pawelkie@ux1.cso.uiuc.edu

Indiana

Culver Summer Camps
1300 Academy Rd., CEF Box 138
Culver, IN 46511
Phone: 800-221-2020/219-842-8207
Fax: 219-842-8462
E-mail: summer@culver1.culver.pvt.k12.

Indiana Golf Academy
1969 Norway Rd.
Monticello, IN 47960
E-mail: bonnell@pwrtl.com

Purdue Boys' and Girls' Golf Camps
Mollenkopf Athletic Center 302A.
Purdue University
West Lafayette, IN 47907-1790
Phone: 317-494-3217

Sam Carmichael's Junior Golf School
Indiana University, Assembly Hall
Bloomington, IN 47405
Phone: 812-855-7950

Tri-State University Golf Camp
300 W. Park St.
Angola, IN 46703
Phone: 219-665-4269
Fax: 219-665-4802

United States Golf Academy
Swan Lake Golf Resort
5203 Plymouth/LaPort Trail
Plymouth, IN 46563
Phone: 219-935-5680/800-582-7534
Fax: 219-935-5087

Iowa

Cyclone Country Golf Camp
P.O. Box 1995
Ames, IA 50010
Phone: 515-232-3999 (6-10pm)
Fax: 515-294-0125

PGA Section Junior Golf Camp
1930 St. Andrews N.E.
Cedar Rapids, IA 52402
Phone: 319-378-9142
Fax: 319-378-9203

University of Iowa Golf Camp
E216 Field House
Iowa City, IA 52242
Phone: 319-335-9714

Kansas

Jayhawk Golf Camp
2104 Inverness Drive
Lawrence, KS 66047
Phone: 913-842-1907/913-842-1714

Kentucky

Murray State University Golf School
Athletic Department
Murray State University
Murray, KY 42071
Phone: 502-762-4895/502-762-4150
Fax: 502-762-3050

Louisiana

Southern Junior Golf Academy
Louisiana State Univ.
Baton Rouge, LA 70808
Phone: 504-383-8714/504-388-8212

Maine

Camp Nashoba North
198 Raymond Hill Rd
Raymond, ME 04071
Phone: 207-655-7170

Camp Wigwam
Harrison, ME 04040
Phone: 207-583-2300
Fax: 207-583-6242
E-mail: wigwam@maine.com

Guaranteed Performance School of Golf
On the Common
Bethel, ME 04217
Phone: 800-654-0125
Fax: 207-824-2233
E-mail: connorsa@nxi.com
URL: http://www.bethelinn.com

Harvey LaMontagne
  Golf Improvement Centers
Paris Hill Country Club
Box 68
Paris, ME 04271
Phone: 207-743-2371

Maryland

Camp Skylemar for Boys
7900 Stevenson Rd.
Balto, MD 21208
Phone: 410-653-2480
Fax: 410-653-1271

Coach Tom Hanna's Playing Camp
22611 Indian Point Road
Bozman, MD 21612
Phone: 301-403-8157/410-745-9119
Fax: 301-403-8366
E-mail: tkhanna@crosslink.net

Jason Rodenhaver Golf School
University of Maryland Golf Course
College Park, MD 20740
Phone: 301-403-4299
Fax: 301-403-4299

Maryland LPGA Girls Club
11500 Carroll Ct.
Upper Marlboro, MD 20772
E-mail: champton@nova.umuc.edu

Massachusetts

Blue Rock Golf School
48 Todd Road
South Yarmouth, MA 02264
Phone: 800-237-8887

Crumpin-Fox Adult Golf Institute
Parmenter Road
Bernardston, MA 01337
Phone: 413-648-9101/800-943-1901
Fax: 413-648-9749

Gillette LPGA Golf Clinics
c/o Jane Blalock Co.
Flagship Wharf, 197 Eighth S
Boston, MA 02129
Phone: 617-242-3100
Fax: 617-242-4884

Golf Learning Center at Firefly
320 Fall River Ave.
Seekonk, MA 02771
Phone: 508-336-6622
Fax: 508-336-6622

Ocean Edge Weekend Golf School
Ocean Edge Resort & Golf Club
832 Villages Dr.
Brewster, MA 02631
Phone: 800-343-6074/508-896-5911
Fax: 508-896-8337

Michigan

Boyne Super Five Golf Week
Boyne Mountain Resort, Boyne Mountain Rd.
Boyne Falls, MI 49713
Phone: 800-GO-BOYNE/616-549-6000
E-mail: info@boyne.com
URL: http://www.boyne.com

Crystal Mountain Golf Schools
12500 Crystal Mountain Dr.
Thompsonville, MI 49683
Phone: 800-968-7686
Fax: 616-378-4594
E-mail: info@crystalmtn.com

Ferris State University Golf Camp
1003 Perry St.
Big Rapids, MI 49307
Phone: 616-592-2213
Fax: 616-592-2135
E-mail: renglish@music.ferris.edu

Golf Academy at The Meadows
4645 W. Campus Dr.
Allendale, MI 49401
Phone: 616-895-1001
E-mail: pbutcher@gvsu.edu
URL: http://www.webgolfer.com/meadows/
  academy1.htm

Katke Golf Camp
Ferris State University
Big Rapids, MI 49307
Phone: 616-592-3765
Fax: 616-592-2135

Michigan Golf Camp of Champions
1000 S. State Street
Ann Arbor, MI 48109-2201
Phone: 313-998-7239
Fax: 313-998-6267

Northern Michigan Golf Academy
McGuire's Resort
P.O. Box 207
Cadillac, MI 49601
Phone: 800-632-7302/616-775-9947
Fax: 616-775-9621

Rick Smith Golf Academy
3962 Wilkinson Rd.
Gaylord, MI 49735
Phone: 800-444-6711/517-732-6711

Women's Golf Academy
539 Cornell
E. Lansing, MI 48823
Phone: 800-WGA-7271/517-332-2195

Minnesota

**Camp Lincoln/Camp Lake Hubert
  Golf Camp**
5201 Eden Circle
Minneapolis, MN 55436
Phone: 800-242-1909/612-922-2545
Fax: 612-922-7149
E-mail: clclh@uslink.net

Minnesota Golf Instructional Camp
516 15th Ave SE
Minneapolis, MN 55455
Phone: 612-625-5863
Fax: 612-624-1326

PGA Section Junior Golf Camp
12800 Bunker Prairie Rd.
Coon Rapids, MN 55448
Phone: 612-754-0820
Fax: 612-754-0891

Rob Hary Junior Golf School
Minnesota Valley Country Club
6300 Auto Club Rd.
Bloomington, MN 55438
Phone: 612-884-1744
Fax: 612-884-2419

Missouri

Heartland Golf Schools
PO Box 410623
St. Louis, MO 63141
Phone: 314-453-0705
E-mail: hgsinc@heartlandgolfschools.co
URL: http://www.heartlandgolfschools.com

PGA Section Junior Golf Camp
P.O. Box 553
Blue Springs, MO 64013
Phone: 816-229-6565

Montana

PGA Section Junior Golf Camp
601 W. Kent Ave.
Missoula, MT 59801
Phone: 406-543-1977

Nevada

Arnold Palmer Golf Academy Oasis
851 Oasis Blvd., P.O. Box 281
Mesquite, NV 89024
Phone: 800-910-2742
Fax: 702-346-7811
URL: http://www.apgaoasis.com

New Hampshire

New Hampshire Tennis & Golf Camp
329 Camp Merrimac Rd.
Contoocook, NH 03229
Phone: 800-TRY-4NHC
Fax: 516-364-8099
E-mail: nhgt@juno.como
URL: http://www.kidscamps.com/specialty/
  sports/

New Jersey

David Glenz Golf Academy
123 Crystal Springs Rd.
Hamburg, NJ 07419
Phone: 888-SWINGFX

Newton's Law of Golf
601 RT. 9 South, Suite B-5
Cape May Court House, NJ 08210
Phone: 609-465-6088
Fax: 609-463-1010

New Mexico

**New Mexico State University
   Professional Golf Management**
Box 30001, Dept. PGM
Las Cruces, NM 88003-8001
Phone: 505-646-2814
Fax: 505-646-1467
E-mail: kefowler@nmsu.edu

PGA Section Junior Golf Camp
2351 Hamilton Road
Alamogordo, NM 88310
Phone: 505-437-0290
Fax: 505-434-5319

**University of New Mexico Lady Lobo
   Golf Camp**
3601 University Blvd. SE
Albuquerque, NM 87131-3046
Phone: 505-277-4527
Fax: 505-277-6222

New York

Hanah International Golf School
Rte. 30
Margaretville, NY 12455
Phone: 800-752-6494/914-586-2100
Fax: 914-586-3104

Holiday Valley Golf School
PO Box 370
Ellicottville, NY 14731
Phone: 716-699-2345
Fax: 716-699-5204

Kutsher's Sports Academy
Anawana Lake Road
Monticello, NY 12701
Phone: 800-724-0238/914-794-5400
Fax: 914-794-0157
E-mail: kutsport@aol.com

**Penn York/Southern Tier Youth
   Golf Camp**
Birch Run Country Club, Birch Run Rd.
Allegany, NY 14706
Phone: 716-373-3113

PGA Section Junior Golf Camp
49 Knollwood Rd., Ste. 200
Elmsford, NY 10523
Phone: 914-347-2416
Fax: 914-347-2014

Roland Stafford Golf School
Box 81
Arkville, NY 12406
Phone: 800-447-8894/914-586-3187
Fax: 914-586-2915
E-mail: golfpro@staffordgolf.com
URL: http://www.staffordgolf.com

Villa Roma Golf School
340 Villa Roma Rd.
Callicoon, NY 12723
Phone: 914-887-5097 (3/25-11/1)
Fax: 914-887-4284

North Carolina

Bertholy-Method Golf School
Paul Bertholy, PO Box One
Foxfire Village, NC 27281
Phone: 910-281-3093

**Bonnie Randolph and Mason Rudolph
   Golf Schools**
High Hampton Inn & Country Club
P.O. Box 338
Cashiers, NC 28717
Phone: 800-334-2551/704-743-2411
Fax: 704-743-5991

Coaches N.C. Golf School
University of North Carolina
P.O. Box 2675
Chapel Hill, NC 27515
Phone: 919-929-1108
Fax: 919-962-0751

Duke University Golf School
Box 90551
Durham, NC 27708
Phone: 919-681-2494/919-681-2288
Fax: 919-681-8612

Jack Lewis Golf Camp
Wake Forest University, P.O. Box 7567
Winston-Salem, NC 27109
Phone: 910-759-6000
Fax: 910-759-6105

Kiski Golf School for Boys and Girls
Duke University Golf Club
Durham, NC 27706
Phone: 919-681-2628

**Marlene Floyd's For Women Only
    Golf Schools**
5350 Club House Ln.
Hope Mills, NC 28348
Phone: 800-637-2694
Fax: 910-323-9606
E-mail: marlenegolf@juno.com

Mid Pines Inn & Golf Club
1010 Midland Road
Southern Pines, NC 28387
Phone: 800-323-2114/919-692-2114
Fax: 919-692-4615

**North Carolina State University
    Wolfpack Golf School**
3000 Ballybunion Way
Raleigh, NC 27613
Phone: 919-846-1536
Fax: 919-846-1543

Pine Needles Lodge & Golf Club
Box 88
Southern Pines, NC 28388
Phone: 800-747-7272
E-mail: pneedles@ac.net
URL: http://www.golflink.net/pineneedles/

Pinehurst Golf Advantage Schools
P.O. Box 4000
Pinehurst, NC 28374
Phone: 910-295-8128/800-795-GOLF
Fax: 919-295-8110

Ohio

Ben Sutton Golf School
P.O. Box 9199
Canton, OH 44711-9199
Phone: 800-225-6923/330-453-4350
Fax: 330-453-8450

**GolfWorks Club Repair, Fitting,
    Assembly, & Business Schools**
4820 Jacksontown Rd., Rte. 13
Newark, OH 43055-7199
Phone: 800-848-8358/614-328-4193
Fax: 614-323-0311

Great Lakes Golf School
25825 Science Park Dr., Ste. 100
Beachwood, OH 44122
Phone: 800-675-1467

Paul Tessler's Progressive Golf School
3781 State Route 5
Newton Falls, OH 44444
Phone: 330-872-7984
Fax: 330-872-7984

Oklahoma

Ball Golf Academy
7501 N. Robinson
Oklahoma City, OK 73116
Phone: 405-842-2626
Fax: 405-340-7529

Mike Holder's Cowboy Golf Camp
Oklahoma State University
1524 Fairway Dr.
Stillwater, OK 74078
Phone: 405-744-7259

Sooner Golf Academy
2305 Creighton
Norman, OK 73071
Phone: 405-364-4875
Fax: 405-325-8021

Tulsa Golf School
Page Belcher Golf Course
6666 S. Union Ave.
Tulsa, OK 74132
Phone: 918-446-1529
Fax: 918-446-6397

Oregon

Balance Point Golf Schools
65278 Stockton Rd.
Enterprise, OR 97828
Phone: 800-898-4563
Fax: 503-426-4863

Pennsylvania

**Bill Mackel's Mini Golf School
    at Cliff Park Inn**
R.R. 4, Box 7200
Milford, PA 18337
Phone: 800-225-6535/717-296-6491
Fax: 717-296-3982

Future Collegians World Tour
609 E. Baltimore Pike
Media, PA 19063
Phone: 888-636-FCWT
Fax: 610-565-0384

Golf School at JKST
P.O. Box 333
Haverford, PA 19041-0333
Phone: 800-TRY-JKST/610-265-9401
Fax: 610-265-3678
E-mail: Adrian@JKST.com
URL: http://www.JKST.com

International Golf School
P.O. Box 15
Berwick, PA 18603
Phone: 717-752-7281

**Penn State Univ. Professional Golf
    Mgmt. Program**
Dept. of Recreation & Park Mgmt.
Penn State, 201
University Park, PA 16802
Phone: 814-863-8987
Fax: 814-863-4257

PGA Section Junior Golf Camp
221 Sherwood Dr.
Monaca, PA 15061
Phone: 412-774-2224

Shippensburg University Golf Camp
CUB, Shippensburg University
Shippensburg, PA 17257
Phone: 717-532-1256

Swing's The Thing Golf Schools
Box 200
Shawnee-on-Delaware, PA 18356
Phone: 800-797-9464/717-421-6666
Fax: 717-476-7517

South Carolina

**Academy of Junior Golf at Furman
    University**
Furman Golf Club, 3300 Poinsett Hwy.
Greenville, SC 29613-0848
Phone: 864-294-9093
Fax: 864-294-8536
E-mail: potter_mic/furman@furman.edu

Arcadian Classic Golf School
701 Hilton Road
Myrtle Beach, SC 29572
Phone: 803-449-5217
Fax: 803-497-9477

Classic Swing Golf School, Inc.
Deer Track Golf Resort, 1705 Platt Blvd.
Surfside Beach, SC 29575
Phone: 800-827-2656/803-650-2545
Fax: 803-650-7977

Golf Academy of Hilton Head Island
P.O. Box 5580
Hilton Head Island, SC 29938
Phone: 800-925-0467/803-785-4540
Fax: 803-785-5116

**Golf Academy of Hilton Head Island
    Junior Masters Program**
P.O. Box 5580
Hilton Head Island, SC 29938
Phone: 800-925-0467/803-785-4540
Fax: 803-785-5116
URL: http://www.golf-academyhhi.com

**Golf Academy of Hilton Head Island
    Junior Masters Summer Pro**
P.O. Box 5580
Hilton Head Island, SC 29938
Phone: 800-925-0467/803-785-4540
Fax: 803-785-5116
URL: http://www.golf-academyhhi.com

Grand Strand Golf Instructions
River Oaks Golf Plantation
831 River Oaks Dr.
Myrtle Beach, SC 29577
Phone: 800-453-6488

Island Golf School
P.O. Box 5372
Hilton Head, SC 29938
Phone: 800-646-5376
Fax: 803-842-9991

Kiawah Island Junior Golf School
Kiawah Island Resort, P.O. Box 1507
Kiawah Island, SC 29457
Phone: 803-768-2121/803-953-1415

Links Group Golf School
P.O. Box 1129
Myrtle Beach, SC 29578
Phone: 800-833-6337
Fax: 803-449-8980
E-mail: linksgroup@aol.com

Myrtle Beach Golf School
P.O. Box 1484
N. Myrtle Beach, SC 29598
Phone: 800-947-9464

Palmetto Dunes Golf School
P.O. Box 5849
Hilton Head Island, SC 29938
Phone: 803-785-1138
Fax: 803-785-1135

Phil Ritson-Mel Sole Golf School
Pawleys Plantation, Hwy. 17
P.O. Box 2580
Pawleys Island, SC 29585
Phone: 800-624-4653/803-237-4993
Fax: 803-237-8397

Tennessee

PGA Section Junior Golf Camp
Golf House Tennessee, 400 Franklin Rd.
Franklin, TN 37069
Phone: 615-790-7600

Tennessee PGA Golf Academy
400 Franklin Rd.
Franklin, TN 37069
Phone: 615-790-7600
Fax: 615-781-0158

Texas

Academy of Golf Dynamics, Inc.
45 Club Estates Pkwy.
Austin, TX 78738
Phone: 800-879-2008/512-261-3300
Fax: 512-261-8168
URL: http://www.moontower.com/golfschl/

Barton Creek Golf Advantage School
8212 Barton Club Dr.
Austin, TX 78735
Phone: 800-336-6157/512-329-4000

Columbia Lakes School of Golf
Columbia Lakes Resort & Conf. Center
188 Freeman Blvd
West Columbia, TX 77486
Phone: 409-345-5151/800-231-1030
Fax: 409-345-3069

Dave Pelz Short Game School
1200 Lakeway Dr., #21
Austin, TX 78734
Phone: 800-833-7370/512-261-6493
Fax: 512-261-5391

**Golfsmith Clubmaker's Training
   Programs**
11000 North IH-35
Austin, TX 78753
Phone: 800-456-3344/512-837-4810
Fax: 512-837-1245

Golfsmith Harvey Penick Golf Academy
11000 N. IH-35
Austin, TX 78753
Phone: 800-477-5869/512-837-4810
Fax: 512-837-9347

Mark Steinbauen Golf Training Center
2301 North Millbend
The Woodlands, TX 77380
Phone: 214-292-4653
Fax: 214-292-7218

**Texas Tech Grad. Golf Workshop
   & Jr. Golf Academy**
Texas Tech University, Box 43011
Lubbock, TX 79409-3011
Phone: 806-742-3335

Utah

Brigham Young University Golf Camps
147 Harman Building
Provo, UT 84602
Phone: 801-378-4851
Fax: 801-378-6361
E-mail: trost@coned1.byu.edu
URL: http://coned.byu.edu/cw/camps/
   main2.htm

Fun International, The Golf School
Emerald River Golf Course
6083 Sweet Basil South
Salt Lake City, UT 84118
Phone: 801-966-7506

Sun Desert Golf Camp
Dixie College, 225 S. 700 East
St. George, UT 84770
Phone: 800-545-4653/801-673-3704
E-mail: durfey@cc.dixie.edu
URL: http://www.dixie.edu/

Vermont

Golf School
Mount Snow Resort
West Dover, VT 05356
Phone: 800-240-2555
Fax: 802-464-4192
URL: http://www.thegolfschool.com/

Stratton Golf School
Stratton Mountain Resort
Stratton Mountain, VT 05155
Phone: 800-238-2424/802-843-6867
Fax: 802-297-2939

Virginia

Green's Folly Golf Camp
1085 Green's Folly Rd.
S. Boston, VA 24592q
Phone: 804-572-4998/3468

Kingsmill Golf Schools
1010 Kingsmill Rd.
Williamsburg, VA 23185
Phone: 800-832-5665/804-253-3906
Fax: 804-253-8246

Tides Inn
P.O. Box 480
Irvington, VA 22480
Phone: 804-438-5501
Fax: 804-438-5222

Wintergreen Golf Academy
Wintergreen Resort, P.O. Box 706
Wintergreen, VA 22958
Phone: 800-325-2200/804-325-8245
URL: http://www.wintergreenresort.com

Washington

Port Ludlow Destination Golf Schools
Port Ludlow Golf & Meeting Retreat
751 Highland D
Port Ludlow, WA 98365
Phone: 800-455-0272/206-437-0272
Fax: 206-437-0637

Wisconsin

Galvano International Golf Academy
Box 626
Wisconsin Dells, WI 53965
Phone: 800-234-6121/800-867-WILD
Fax. 608-254-4085

Grand Geneva Golf School
Highway 50 East
Lake Geneva, WI 53147
Phone: 414-248-2556
Fax: 414-248-3192